The Samurai of Sales

THE
SAMURAI
OF
SALES

The Path to TRUE
Sales Mastery

MITCH HARRIS

NEW YORK

LONDON • NASHVILLE • MELBOURNE • VANCOUVER

The Samurai of Sales

The Path to True Sales Mastery

© 2019 Mitch Harris

Published in New York, New York, by Morgan James Publishing. Morgan James is a trademark of Morgan James, LLC. www.MorganJamesPublishing.com

The Morgan James Speakers Group can bring authors to your live event. For more information or to book an event visit The Morgan James Speakers Group at www.TheMorganJamesSpeakersGroup.com.

ISBN 9781614482505 paperback
ISBN 9781614488613 case laminate
ISBN 9781614482512 eBook
Library of Congress Control Number: 2012933212

Cover Design by:
Rachel Lopez
www.r2cdesign.com

Interior Design by:
Chris Treccani
www.3dogcreative.net

In an effort to support local communities, raise awareness and funds, Morgan James Publishing donates a percentage of all book sales for the life of each book to Habitat for Humanity Peninsula and Greater Williamsburg.

Get involved today! Visit
www.MorganJamesBuilds.com

"One should not be envious of someone who has prospered by unjust deeds. Nor should he disdain someone who has fallen while adhering to the path of righteousness."
—IMAGAWA SADAYO *(1325-1420)*

CONTENTS

FOREWORD

Have you ever wondered what separates the top producing sales pros on the planet from the masses and how they got to that position in the first place?

Why is it that certain people or entire organizations seem to be able to consistently close more business and initiate career-changing relationships, while others seem to be in a perpetual state of struggle? I've always found this question to be intriguing and I've always been impressed by people who are able to answer it.

Mitch Harris is one of those people. He has been helping companies in many industries to elevate their sales performance and bottom line production for close to two decades. I have personally known Mitch for over seven years and the impact he has had on the people he works with has been amazing. He has a knack and a true love for identifying what needs to be improved and how, while teaching incredibly powerful sales methodologies and approaches that have made **the pivotal difference**.

In *The Samurai of Sales*, Mitch imparts that wisdom in a way that I believe can be a true game changer for anyone looking to elevate their sales performance. Whether you're relatively new in your particular industry or a twenty-year veteran. Whether you're an account executive who wants to improve your personal production, a sales manager looking to help your team improve or the company owner, *The Samurai of Sales* is a must read!

The parallels Mitch draws between the Samurai and what it takes to be a modern day sales master are profound, yet easy to understand. And while he shares his philosophy on sales mastery and the mindset you need to thrive in today's evolving sales climate, he also teaches specific tools and methods that you can use to execute day to day in the real world, immediately.

I believe reading this book and applying its lessons will have a profound, lasting impact on your career and your life overall. Enjoy and as Mitch would say, God Bless, best of luck and go close some business!

David L. Hancock
Guerilla Marketing International Advisory Board Chair

ACKNOWLEDGMENTS

It's simple—without the people mentioned below this book would not have been possible. When you're getting value from the pages that follow and perhaps you are feeling thankful for having a chance to read this book, I ask you to consider these folks.

I'd like to thank my friend and mentor Bob Quintana ("Q") for giving me wings in this industry and showing me how the system works—as well as being the first to teach me so many of the tools and principles I now teach others. And we've remained great friends to this day. I'd also like to thank Tony Robbins for being my first introduction to personal growth and professional development. You showed me what was possible Tony. You made me realize that the future really was in my hands and you gave me the tools on how to do it.

My deepest gratitude to Mark Chin. Mark, you helped give me the confidence and critical answers I needed when I was just starting out. My warmest thanks to Jeff and Len Kurzweil who helped me to transform my company from a vision into a reality and for all of the non-judgmental support and patience while I was figuring things out. And to Jeff in particular for your amazing friendship. My thanks to Jeff Spurgeon as well for your amazing friendship and support.

I'd like to thank David Hancock and Rick Frishman at Morgan James Publishing for their support, patience and visionary leadership while I was working out all of the kinks and making this book a reality. My thanks to Tiffany Gibson as well for her support and effort in making this happen.

I'd like to thank Mark Victor Hansen for being the expansive presence that he is and reminding me that completing a book and getting it out there was meant to happen for me. Your wisdom has been invaluable to me, Mark.

I want to thank Barbara Dangellis for her beautiful heart energy, for being the voice of spirit when I needed to hear it and for inspiring and encouraging me at a most crucial juncture in my life.

Thank you Father for teaching me to stick to things even when I don't feel like it and for giving me the mental toughness I have had to call upon when the going has been rough.

And most of all, I want to truly thank my mother for breathing life into me and being the most amazing mother a human being could hope to have. Mother, when I was on the brink and face-to-face with the abyss, you were there holding firmly, making sure I was okay. For that I am forever in your debt. I love you.

WARNING —DISCLAIMER

This book is designed to provide information on effective communication, selling and business development skills. It is sold with the understanding that the publisher and author are not engaged in rendering legal, accounting or other professional services. If legal or other expert assistance is required, the services of a competent professional should be sought.

It is not the purpose of this book to reprint all of the information that is otherwise available to sales professionals and entrepreneurs, but instead to complement, amplify and supplement other texts. You are urged to read all the available material, learn as much as possible about selling skills and business development and tailor the information to your individual needs.

The Samurai of Sales is not a get-rich-quick scheme. Anyone who decides to enter or continue a career in any branch of professional sales must expect to invest a lot of time and effort into it. For many people, professional sales is a very lucrative and rewarding industry. For others, it never quite pans out and provides minimal if any income.

In addition, reference to the ancient Samurai practice of Seppuku, or honorable suicide in no way endorses the practice or even consideration of suicide. It is simply used to illustrate the Samurai's commitment to excellence and honor. If you are considering hurting yourself in any way and for any reason, we strongly recommend that you receive professional help.

Every effort has been made to make this book as complete and accurate as possible. However, there may be mistakes, both typographical and in content. Therefore, this text should be used only as a general guide and not as the ultimate source of sales mastery and effective business development.

Furthermore, this book contains information on selling skills, effective communication and business development that is current only up to the printing date.

The purpose of this book is to educate and entertain. The author and Communication Mastery shall have neither liability nor responsibility to any person or entity with respect to any loss or damage caused, or alleged to have been caused, directly or indirectly, by the information contained in this book.

If you do not wish to be bound by the above, you may return this book to the publisher for a full refund.

INTRODUCTION

As far as how the pages you're about to read relate to my experience and what I have to teach you in this book, it's actually rather simple: ***If I can do it, you can too!***

I began in the world of professional sales over twenty-five years ago.

When I first started, I knew I was going to be great because other people had told me so. I was well spoken, I had college training, I was outgoing, full of ambition and drive, hardworking and willing to learn. *Of course* I was going to be great at sales.

It took me about ninety days to realize that those people were absolutely wrong!

After a shaky start in the office solutions industry, where I worked for a Fortune 500 corporation, selling copier and fax machines door to door in midtown Manhattan, I entered the investment banking industry as a stockbroker trainee. Let me clarify—a *full service, retail* stockbroker trainee.

What that means is I was on the phone making cold calls an average of ten hours a day, taking rapid-fire rejection from potential investors all over the country who didn't know me from Adam and didn't want to speak with me. I was averaging about six hundred dials and thirty pitches per day.

Most trainees just couldn't handle that kind of intensity and were out of the business in ninety days or less. Let me repeat: ninety days—or less! I hit the ninety-day wall and had nothing to show for it either. To make matters worse, I just wasn't ... good. There were people I was working with, side by side, who I felt were no more intelligent than I was, but who were getting *much* better results in a much shorter time. They knew how to get people to say *yes*. They somehow had it figured out. I did not.

It was frustrating to say the least.

But I'm no stranger to hard work and there are those who would say I've got some backbone. So I decided to dig my toes in the sand, work my tail off for two years, and learn the industry. And two years into the process, with a tremendous amount of hard work and sacrifice under my belt, the bottom line was that *I was no further along than I was at day one!*

I was twenty-five years of age and had been out of college for over four years. I had a series-seven and series-three license under my belt and had worked virtually the entire time, but my profile wasn't exactly inspiring: I was still living at home with Mom in Brooklyn where I grew up (after we moved from Queens), and I was earning a stipend of $250 per week. I had no car, no life, and was barely making ends meet. I rarely traveled out of the city, let alone the state. *Not exactly the profile I was looking for.*

But in many ways, that situation was the best thing that could have happened to me. Because it was at that point that I made a **decision.** And there is an incredible feeling of power and freedom in doing that. I am not talking about simply deciding in spirit, or theory. I mean making a *firm, ironclad commitment* to take action on something and see it through to its conclusion.

I made a decision to step into a process that forever changed my life and that continues to this day. It led me to become the prodigal student. I began to read, listen to and train alongside some of the best teachers in the world in the areas of professional sales and personal development. Individuals like: Tony Robbins, Brian Tracy, Zig Zigler, Tom Hopkins, Chin Ning Chu, Napolean Hill, Og Mandino, Les Brown, Harvey Mackay, T. Harv Eker, Bob Quintana, Blair Singer, Howard Rackover, Jay Abraham, Jay Conrad Levinson, Robert Shook and many more.

I consumed everything I could—books, tapes, videos, live seminars, tele- courses, webinars, coaching, you name it. There are certain seminars I have attended over ten times. There are certain audio recordings I have listened to over one hundred times! I practiced, rehearsed, memorized, repeated, applied and continued the process. I was on a mission!

Now, I am not going to tell you there was a magic bullet that changed everything overnight. I will also confess that I am not necessarily the fastest learner on the planet. But I will say that over the course of roughly eighteen months, I went from the profile described above—broke and still living with Mom—to getting a check in one month that was worth more than the average American was earning in a year!

I went from being a no-name in the boardroom to being asked consistently to give the sales meetings or to train brokers who were twenty or thirty years my senior in the industry. And I took on the unofficial role of mentor and advisor to many. But I'm not just talking about monetary or professional progress here. I'm also referring to the shift in confidence, identity, and lifestyle that took place within me as well.

Before I knew it, I was traveling all around the country, and then I was on a plane to Costa Rica taking a much-needed vacation—*because I could!* I had quickly developed a bit of a following of people who wanted to learn from and emulate me. I moved into Manhattan, bought the things I wanted, began frequenting some of the finest restaurants in the city (which I still do), and much, much more.

In addition, I gained the confidence of knowing that from that point forward, I could always write my own ticket as an entrepreneur, and that I would not have to be at the mercy of circumstances around me—I could forge my own path to success. I had honed my skills. I had become a true **Samurai Of Sales.** It was a *huge* shift in a relatively short time. Anyone who has been through that shift knows exactly what I'm talking about. And let me tell you, it's a rather incredible feeling.

That process continued to the point where people began to request my services as a consultant, trainer and executive coach. I finally got into the business of doing exactly that. In 2002, I created my own consulting and executive coaching organization called **Communication Mastery.** And we have had a tremendous impact on both individuals and organizations all over the country and from many different industries.

We have helped individuals to improve their selling skills, their time management and leadership abilities, their levels of confidence, and—of course—their bottom line **results.** In addition, we have helped organizations to completely reinvent themselves, cultivate record-breaking sales teams, develop entire sales processes and systems, transform corporate culture, and so much more. We are now having an impact on a massive scale.

I've worked with clients in all shapes and sizes and at all levels of skill and experience. I've helped the struggling rookie (as I once was) to achieve that ever- so-critical breakthrough and turn the corner. I've helped veteran account executives climb back into the six-figure (and in some cases seven-figure) bracket and attain greatness once again.

I've helped the experienced sales manager—who couldn't seem to find the answers and was waffling—to step back into gear and double or triple his team's production. And I've helped the company president or managing director to run more effective meetings, reinvigorate corporate culture, and create a more cohesive organization. And the beautiful thing is that I've been able to deliver consistently!

I've created tools as well: books, like the one you are reading right now; audio programs; tele-courses; video programs; online resources; networking groups; masterminds; personal coaching services, and more. It has been quite a journey!

And throughout this process, I have developed methods, approaches, and systems that are designed specifically to assist the contemporary sales professional in becoming more effective and generating better results— to be able to get the business where the competition won't. Many of the principles that I share are not new, because I've got news for you: whether you like it or not, the fundamentals do not change! (Regardless of what the latest flash in the pan might say).

Something Jim Rohn once said about fundamentals always stuck with me. *"The thing you have to remember about fundamentals is there are no new fundamentals."* Let that be perhaps the first tip you take from this book.

But while the principles may not change, the most effective ways to *approach* and *implement* do. Markets, societies, and industries are always evolving. The needs, mindset, and concerns of the contemporary consumer are more complex than ever!

And in today's day and age of the internet, social media, email campaigns, blogs, online video and more–with everyone speaking about mass marketing and going viral–there still is not and never will be a substitute for being able to cultivate great, one-on-one client relationships with the right decision makers.

The ability to connect and dialogue in a way that has them want to give you the business is paramount. Getting someone's attention through your marketing efforts is one thing. Being able to convert that prospect into a great long term and even life long client is another skill entirely.

The strategies I share in this book have been tried, tested, and proven out there in the real world where the champs get separated from the chumps rather quickly. They are fresh and cutting edge. An attempt at success in any branch of sales would be futile without these strategies in your toolbox. And I share them in my own unique style and from my own unique perspective.

THE SAMURAI

I am not a scholar of Japanese history. Nor do I claim to have a deep understanding of the samurai or what they stood for. But from what I have come to understand about how the samurai lived, I can tell you without question that they are one of the best examples in human history of what it takes to become a true master.

When developing your skills as a sales professional, if your goal is to acquire *true mastery*, there is inherently a certain lifestyle, focus, and overall philosophy you must adhere to—as did the samurai.

Allow me to clarify. I am *not* talking about simply learning a few techniques or just getting better—which is fine if that's your goal. I am talking about attaining true *mastery*: integration on a deep, cellular level; walking around with the poise and confidence of a true *closer;* knowing that if it is at all humanly possible to create the transaction, you are going to be the one who does it. It's knowing that if *you* can't get it done, *no one* can get it done. You perform feats of talent, skill, and proficiency that amaze even experienced veterans.

Why shoot for anything less in a profession that has so much to offer you?

This is my perspective when coaching and training my clients. So you can bet this perspective permeates the pages you are about to read as well.

The samurai were impressive indeed. As many modern scholars and historians frequently reference, the samurai lived according to a code called **"Bushido,"** also known as "the way of the warrior." Loosely translated into Western terms, this could be defined as *chivalry.* It stressed frugality, loyalty, martial arts mastery, and honor until death. Bushido wasn't so much a strict written code as it was a collective understanding that was cultivated and passed down from generation to generation.

Bushido is comprised of seven primary **virtues**. They are defined as:

Rectitude (義 *gi)*
Courage (勇 *yuu)*
Benevolence (仁 *jin)*
Respect (礼 *rei)*
Honesty (誠 *makoto or* 信 *shin*)
Honor (誉 *yo)*
Loyalty (忠 *chuu)*

The samurai's life was committed to mastery. Anything less was considered shameful. He would spend most of his waking hours either in some form of service or in some form of training.

This is not to say that the samurai did not find time for enjoyment and pleasure. This too is a part of life. But overall, the levels of focus, discipline and self-cultivation the samurai adhered to on a consistent basis have found little parallel.

What a great archetype for what is possible and what it takes to achieve true mastery in any endeavor! And I want to point out that while the samurai in days past were male, the essence I refer to here applies to *women* just as well as it does to men. I am talking about the state of mind, spirit, and philosophy that the samurai embodied. Loosely translated from Japanese, samurai means "those who serve." In today's day and age, those qualities are not the sovereign domain of men only.

And to be clear, when I say "warrior," I don't mean someone who is always fighting and killing others, which is a common misconception of the word in today's society. True, there are times when a warrior is engaged in such activities. But what I mean here is someone who is vigorous in her pursuit of mastery and accomplishment—someone who gives full effort and intensity to achieving greatness at what she is engaged in, and who attains results that truly set the standard for her craft. And finally, a warrior is someone who embraces the process of addressing his personal barriers and anything that could possibly stand between him and the result he desires.

Two glaring facts stand out when considering the samurai archetype:

1. As a group, and on the whole, the samurai actually adhered to these virtues and lived their lives accordingly. Their values weren't simply empty words used in times of exultation and praise.
2. These were real people who actually existed—they are not some fictional creation.

A large part of my life's work is teaching and coaching others in the pursuit of their own self-mastery. Thus the name of my company: **Communication Mastery.** *Communication* refers not only to external communication with others, but also to internal communication with oneself.

Internal communication is inner harmony, self-trust, and self-knowing. It is how well you honor your word to *yourself,* and the quality of your thoughts and beliefs, behavior and habits. The questions you ask yourself and your ability to follow through in times of difficulty. In my opinion, knowing who you are and being true to yourself are perhaps life's two greatest virtues.

I take that philosophy and approach to anything I teach. Personal transformation is a *holistic* process. If you want any individual part of the self to improve, you must consider the self as a whole when going through the process.

In my process of comparing the samurai to a true sales master, many parallels leapt out at me:

- It is clearly the road less traveled.
- It requires intense discipline and a commitment to ongoing training at an extremely high level.
- You must continually work to maintain your edge.

- Some practitioners have more natural ability than others, but you don't have to be a natural to attain mastery.
- When you have attained mastery, the benefits are tremendous. You carry yourself with a confidence few others possess.
- You hold yourself to a much higher standard than the majority could ever fathom.
- You are most effective and truly in your power when coming from a place of service.
- There is a small group of truly elite masters that even other masters look up to and emulate.
- You possess the ability to perform feats and achieve results that astound even experienced veterans.
- You possess the ability to have an immediate and lasting impact on people, situations and entire communities.
- You can completely change someone's perspective and feelings on a particular topic within seconds.
- Your skills can be used as a force for good and noble intent, or a force for evil and wrongdoing.
- You choose to walk the noble path.
- There are others who posses the levels of skill and insight you do, but they are few and far between. And you can usually spot one of them immediately.

I encourage you to review this material as often as you feel is necessary to gain mastery—as I once did and still do. Because remember, *mastery is not a destination; it is a **process***.

If you would like to send me your thoughts or have me come speak to your organization after reading this book or listening to the audio program, I would love to hear from you. Thank you very much for giving me your time and trust in choosing to read *The Samurai of Sales* and perhaps some time in the not-so- distant future we will have an opportunity to meet in person.

I leave you with one question. *What are you committed to creating for yourself and the people you truly care for?* In other words, what will becoming a much more successful sales professional or entrepreneur give you the opportunity to enjoy? Let that be the guiding force in going through these life-changing pages. Thank you very much and enjoy!

Mitchell J. Harris

Mitch Harris
The Samurai of Sales

CONDITIONING YOUR MIND TO STAY THE COURSE

STAYING IN THE GAME IS MORE IMPORTANT THAN ANYTHING ELSE

"It is the very mind itself that leads the mind astray; of the mind, do not be mindless."
—UESHIBA

THE SINGLE MOST IMPORTANT INGREDIENT FOR SALES MASTERY

I will lay it out for you very simply. This comes from over twenty years of studying, learning from and training with some of the most talented sales professionals on the planet—and blazing my own path as well:

The single most important ingredient that separates those who achieve the results they're committed to from those who do not, is the ability of the former to effectively manage their states of mind and emotion — and to do this consistently, in a way that allows them to follow through and stay the course in the face of whatever is thrown at them.

1

There you have it. Whether they are getting the results they want or not, whether things are going well or to the contrary, top performers are able to maintain a certain level of focus, follow-through and resiliency that gets them to their destination.

If you want the prize, whatever it may be, you *must* direct the focus of your mind, and you must condition yourself to stay the course. Any skill, tool, or approach I teach you will mean very little or nothing if you do not possess the mindset necessary to stay the course and follow through. This is beyond important.

WHAT IS YOUR MIND?

This brings us to a question that is often avoided by those who teach mind management. And that is: *What is your mind?* Upon first reading this, you may say to yourself, "Wow, that's a pretty broad question!"

You hear many teachers talk about how important it is to manage your states of mind on a consistent basis—and of course, it is critical. But wouldn't you agree that if you're going to talk about managing *anything* effectively, especially something as important to your success as your own mind, it would serve you to be clear on exactly what it is you're talking about?

As I so often do, I'd like to first reference Webster's definition:

> *"Mind: The seat of consciousness, in which thinking, feeling, etc. takes place."*

Interesting. I'd say the word "etc." in this definition is used to cover a rather broad array of experience. Yes?

I'd like to share my own working definition of what is meant by "the mind." I would like to emphasize that this is what *I* have concluded, based on my own experience. This does not, by any means, have to be your definition or what you accept as the truth. And if it is not, I encourage you to do some searching and exploration of your own to get clear on your definition of this critical topic.

I do *not* perceive your mind to be simply your brain, which seems to be a rather common misconception. It uses elements or faculties of your brain most of the time, but your mind is not strictly your brain. The brain is a tool that the mind uses. The brain is the engine, the factory, the storage center, and the control room for a lot of what the mind is up to, but it is not your mind.

The brain is made up of functions, information, connections, impulses, message centers, etc., which allow you to carry out the intended actions that the mind delivers. The brain is a physical and chemical bridge, if you will, for the mind to operate through.

When I talk about the mind, I am referring to **that entire experience of *thought, emotion, feeling, memory, intention, identity, intellect* and *skill*, that contributes to who you are, how you function, and how you experience life.** You may want to read that definition again. Please notice I did not say that the mind "defines" who you are, or that it "is" who you are; I said it *contributes* to who you are.

There have been many teachers throughout the millennia and up to the modern day, from various disciplines, who have taught that you are much more than your mind, and that your mind is simply one part of your being—it is a tool to be managed. I am inclined to agree with them.

The mind is *affected* by the brain, and vice versa; but the mind is so much more than just the brain. Likewise, the mind is affected by the body and vice versa, but it is also so much more than just the body. It is those two elements— the brain and the body—combined, as well as a third, more intangible element, which some call spirit, some call God, and some call intuition. These elements together make up and affect what we refer to as the mind.

So when we talk about the mind, we're talking about a very broad experience. Of course, I don't claim to completely understand how it all works. If you can figure that one out, you will have solved one of life's great mysteries.

WHAT IT MEANS TO MANAGE YOUR STATES OF MIND

So what specifically do I mean by managing your states of mind and emotion on a consistent basis? Well, what I mean by that is the following:

1. When in action and working towards a certain outcome or result, being able to keep yourself focused on what is *most* important and what is *most* productive —on a *consistent* basis.

2. To be able to *endure*—to stay the course, or stay on track—in the face of the inevitable setbacks, adversities and frustrations that will come up in your life when you're working towards anything worthwhile or meaningful.

3. Not to be stopped when things don't go your way, or when things aren't "fair."

4. To be totally focused, clear, and in the zone when you are in those key, clutch moments that require you to perform at your best; where you seem to have the right things to say and the right questions to ask—the right ideas roll off of your tongue effortlessly.

5. To maintain habits and patterns of behavior that develop rock-solid character and set you up to follow through and win on a consistent basis. To avoid the inconsistent behaviors or ongoing procrastination that can block you from your desired outcomes.

6. While of course life has its ups and downs—and feeling down from time to time is a part of the process—being able to experience down-times much less frequently and to move through them more smoothly. This means you get back on track more quickly and easily, and you are at your best more often. By "your best," I mean you are in that state of mind where you truly feel on top of your game and **unstoppable.** You just know you can't be beat, and you know how to stay in that place most of the time.

7. And finally, to be able to truly enjoy and appreciate your accomplishments—perhaps being willing to give yourself credit on a more consistent basis. Likewise, to be able to appreciate and

enjoy your *setbacks* as well. Yes, you read that correctly. View your setbacks as valuable learning experiences that teach and help you develop as a human being, not as end-of-the-world disasters that totally define who you are or what you're capable of. To squeeze deeply the juice out of life and enjoy it for everything it's worth!

So is this important? You better believe it!

I'm going to shed a bit of light on some approaches that have been proven, time and time again, to be effective at accomplishing what I've described above. Some I have come up with on my own; some were suggested by others who came before me, and others are a combination of the two. In other words, the latter are ideas or principles that were around long before me, which I have improved, updated, or developed in a way that makes them more relevant and helps them land much more powerfully—especially in regards to mastering your sales game.

WHY COMMIT TO MANAGING YOUR MIND?

When talking about managing your states of mind, another critical question comes up: *why?* Why commit to managing your states of mind and emotion on a consistent basis? In other words, why even bother, especially if you're already doing well?

To pose a question like this to a samurai would have been laughable. To *not* continually work on conditioning one's mind and one's skills would not even occur to him. It would have been like asking him to imagine life without breath.

I think of the mind as being like an elephant. This is a metaphor I once heard in a discourse given by my meditation mentor, S.N. Goenka. The elephant is this huge, powerful animal with incredible strength and potential. If left wild and untamed, it is capable of inflicting incredible damage and destruction on almost anything in its path. It could certainly crush a human being with ease, and there have been cases in the past where that has happened.

But if trained and effectively disciplined, an elephant can be used as an awesome tool to accomplish great tasks, move incredibly heavy objects, transport people or things, and even to become a weapon of defense in times of war, which used to be the case in some parts of the world.

Likewise, the mind too is an incredible resource with what many believe is unlimited potential. Very often, when left to its own devices, it can be incredibly destructive and harmful, leading us down paths we'd rather not go. Yet when trained, disciplined, and directed with purpose, it can perform incredible tasks and accomplish the most amazing results.

Furthermore, you want to manage your mind because the degree to which you *don't* is the degree to which your success, follow-through and execution will be unpredictable and in doubt; because there is a huge difference between *knowing* what to do and *doing* what you know, just as there is between common sense and common practice; and because anything you know—anything you understand or may be skilled at— will only be as useful, effective, and *profitable* as the degree to which you actually take it out there into the world and *use it*.

That execution, follow-through, and ability to finish the job is as important as any other part of the success process. Doesn't that just make sense? As someone once said to me years ago:

> *"Don't just accept something because I say it.*
> *Ask yourself if it makes sense and decide for yourself."*

THE PAIN/PLEASURE PRINCIPLE

So let's take a closer look at the topic of managing your mind. The first thing I want to talk about is critical—I repeat, *critical*—if you are even going to even *think* about managing your states of mind and emotion on a consistent basis. This is a concept that's been around for many years; it's been taught, used and practiced by so many individuals and called by so many different names that I couldn't even begin to give credit to whomever it actually originated from.

It's been called neuro-linguistic programming ("NLP"), neuro-associative conditioning, neuro-conditioning, neuro-programming, and associative conditioning. Unfortunately, this methodology has been the topic of debate between many people as far as who actually created it and who deserves the credit. My instinct is to point first and foremost to the Buddha over 2,500 years ago (which is not a common reference), when he spoke about embracing pain and suffering as a reality and a part of life, and working through that as a path towards enlightenment.

But in a more modern and perhaps secular context (although I have never considered Buddhism to be a religion)—and in regards to the personal growth and development aspect of it specifically—I would point to Richard Bandler and Mike Grinder as having founded this methodology, and to Mr. Tony Robbins for bringing it to the masses on a global scale. He was the first person I ever heard speaking about it.

You can call it "ham on rye conditioning" if you like. But whatever you wish to call it, I share it with you because it is effective, extremely powerful and it alone can make a *huge* difference in how successful you are at conditioning your mind and developing habit patterns that drive you towards that which you desire.

I'd like to direct your attention to one of the foundational tenets of this methodology. I call it **"the pain/pleasure principle."** The basic premise of the pain/pleasure principle is as follows: If you boil being successful down to its essence —having what you want out of life and enjoying the process—then taking the actions necessary to make this happen really isn't very complicated. It's actually rather simple. I'm not saying it's always easy, but it *is* simple.

It's a matter of first knowing what you want; in other words, what your intended outcome is. Then it's a matter of taking the actions necessary to achieve it. Once you're in action, you simply need to observe if what you're doing is working, or if you need to change your approach. Once you're taking the right actions towards achieving your result, you simply stay on track and continue to do the things that work until you've achieved it.

Pretty simple—yes?

So here's the question—and it's a question that was posed to me years ago and is one that changed my life, which is why I'd like to pose it to you.

If it's so simple, why doesn't everybody do it?

Bad breaks and bumps in the road included (which we'll talk about later on), if achieving success and the things you want in life really is that simple, why don't more people do it? Why don't more people take the actions necessary to make it happen?

Another way of asking this question is: *what, more than anything else, holds people back from really going for it in life?*

Yes, you're correct: the answer to that, I would assert, is **fear.** I say you're correct because whenever I conduct workshops or seminars and ask that question, the first answer that comes to mind for the overwhelming majority of people is "fear." And it is absolutely correct. Webster defines fear as **"anxiety caused by real or possible danger."** Fear holds us back, and in some cases it paralyzes us from following through and taking action.

Now, that may have been a relatively simple answer. But here's an even more interesting question.

Fear of what?

You may say fear of failure. You may say fear of success. Some might say fear of embarrassment or humiliation, and others might say fear of being let down or disappointed—and that is all correct, depending on the individual.

But all factors considered, the one word I would use to describe what we're afraid of overall is **pain.** The pain/pleasure principle simply states that ultimately people are driven by two forces—either their *need to avoid pain or their desire to gain pleasure.* These two forces literally drive human behavior and dictate the actions we take—or don't take.

Let's take cold-calling or prospecting—getting new contacts or prospects into your pipeline—as an example. I am *extremely* confident that if you ask the overwhelming majority of salespeople in any industry, they would agree that prospecting for new clients is an extremely important part of their business, and that at a certain point—especially at the beginning of your career—if you do not prospect, your pipeline of potential business will diminish dramatically and may even dry up completely.

Well, if that's the case, *why don't all salespeople cold-call and prospect like complete maniacs?* If they know that it makes sense and that it will give them the results they want, why don't they do it more often?

It is because they associate *pain* with taking that action. They associate pain with reaching out to new prospects and hearing the word *"no!"*

Why? Because they define the word "no" as rejection, as failure, as inadequacy, or a slew of other painful emotions. They think that if they hear "no," it reflects upon them personally, and they may be afraid of being judged and classified as just another salesperson. And while taking no action may not give them the results they want, it's certainly more pleasurable or less painful than dealing with the rejection in that moment.

You may say to yourself, "Well, if they took the actions, they could get those results and experience the pleasure of those results." That might be true, but what's more real for them is the present moment, and the possibility of the pain of being rejected or of hearing the word "no."

Let's take taxes as a more general example. I'm sure you would agree that logically it just makes sense to handle your taxes well in advance of the deadline in April. Yet every year, the majority of Americans wait until the last minute to address this critical aspect of life, let alone get it handled. You have people rushing to get it in just in time. The lines at the post office are jammed the day before taxes are due. People have to send their mail certified, in order to document that it was sent on time, and yet still many people request extensions.

Why does this happen? Because up until the last minute, most people associate dealing with the necessary paperwork and reviewing their financial life with this experience we call *pain*. Maybe they view it as a hassle. Maybe it reminds them of how much money they are *not* making or how much they will have to pay in taxes. Who knows? But at the last minute, the thought of not getting it done and all of the consequences that would ensue is even more painful, and so they push through and get it done.

Be aware of what you link pain to and what you link pleasure to, because it is extremely important. It can determine what actions you take or don't take, the quality of your follow through, and—ultimately—the results you achieve in your life. The beauty of this is that with proper training and repetition, you can actually *re-condition what you link pain and pleasure to!* As incredible as it sounds, it is possible. I know, because I've done it in my own life.

This is also very effective because it allows you to go past the mindset of just "disciplining" yourself, which is the attempt to use the guise of strict willpower to force-feed your mind into taking on things it associates with pain. For example, how effective are the crash diets where you just force yourself to eat foods you don't enjoy, without any balance or rewards built into the process?

Well, I'm here to tell you that with diets like that, even if the person has succeeded in losing a certain amount of weight, they will more often than not find the weight loss to be temporary, and eventually they fall off the diet, put the weight back on, and become even heavier than they were before they started the diet in the first place! You may have even had this experience yourself once or twice—or twelve times.

That's because your mind will resist what it associates pain with, because the need to avoid pain is *biological*. It's a defense mechanism that we were given long ago, to keep us from doing stupid things that could hurt us. For example, one of the things that keeps you from sticking your hand in fire is the fact that when you do so, it's extremely painful. That sensation alone is usually enough to guarantee you won't be doing it again. Studies have shown that the fear of emotional pain can be just as intense, if not *more* intense, than the fear of physical pain—your body reacts the same way.

Unfortunately, through the course of human experience, we can distort that mechanism in a way that doesn't always serve us. In other words, we may associate *pain* with things that are good for us and *pleasure* with things that could be detrimental or unproductive. Have you ever noticed yourself running from success or avoiding the actions you know you should be taking, or engaging in things like self-sabotage or erratic behavior and you're not quite sure why? It's because on some level in your mind, you are linking a sense of pain to doing those things that will serve you, and pleasure to avoiding them.

Yes, it is a simple approach to analyzing human behavior, but in my experience I have found it to be absolutely accurate.

Let me ask you this: do you see how strongly this principle can affect your life? I have some blunt questions to ask you. They may not be the easiest questions to read as you go through them, because they may remind you of areas you still need to improve. But they are *vitally important* to identifying how this pain/pleasure principle may be playing a role in the quality of your life and particularly in your success as a sales professional and entrepreneur. I encourage you to put some time aside for this and treat it like an exercise.

Take a candid, blunt, and rigorous review of your behavior and of how you consistently operate your business.

- Do you tend to procrastinate or avoid prospecting, cold-calling or making new contacts, even when you know it will serve you to make those contacts?
- Do you, likewise, tend to procrastinate and/or avoid contacting warm-market relationships?
  — Sometimes these can be even more difficult, because there is history and expectations already embedded into these relationships.
- Do you tend to schedule consecutive appointments that always seem to be geographically far away from each other or on opposite ends of your sales territory?
- Do you feel awkward—or feel like you are doing something inappropriate—when you ask people for referrals?

- If you have asked for referrals and just gotten one or two, do you feel you are pushing the envelope or wearing out your welcome if you ask for more?

- Do you tend to feel nervous or uncomfortable when it is time to challenge a prospect on his concerns, objections, or reasons for not wanting to do business with you?

- Do you tend to feel nervous or afraid when it is time to ask for the money, ask for the order, or move the transaction to a close? Do you feel somehow as if you're crossing a line you shouldn't?

- Do you believe that overall, salespeople are a pretty one-dimensional group that don't really care about their customers and just want to make a buck? Not that **you** would do that of course, but salespeople in general?

- Do you tend to avoid asking for help or support when it would clearly be the wise thing to do? Do you have more trouble asking for help than giving it?

- Do you tend to become nervous or afraid when handling larger deals and proposals, verses medium or small sized deals?

- Do you tend to become nervous or intimidated when dealing with higher or senior-level decision makers (in other words, the people you really should be speaking to) verses mid- or lower-level players?

- Do you find that you end up falling into the role of friend or conversationalist more than sales professional or consultant when dealing with prospects? Do you have great conversations, but no (or little) conversion into results?

- Do you doubt your desire, worthiness, or ability to be in professional sales in the first place?

If you answered *"yes"* to even one of these questions, let alone several or all of them, you *definitely* have some pain/pleasure connections to sales-related activities that are holding you back!

If you did *not* answer "yes" to even one of these questions, you are by far the exception; but just to be clear, you may want to review them again. It is not uncommon for people in professional sales, even experienced veterans with proven results, to have some limiting pain/pleasure associations.

But if, after thorough observation, you really did not answer "yes" to even one, then kudos to you. This is one aspect of sales mastery you need not concern yourself with—*for now!* But read on, my friend. There is plenty more to take in and learn.

Any samurai who would go into battle with only one skill or tool of defense in place would surely be inviting defeat.

If you did answer "yes" to one or more of the questions above, I have two more simple questions for you:

1. **What impact are those limiting pain/pleasure associations having on your behavior and, consequently, your results and your personal income?**
2. **Are you willing to do what is necessary to recondition your mind for success in those and other areas?**

In the next chapter, "Your Beliefs: The Pain/Pleasure Navigator," you will gain more clarity regarding what specifically causes you to associate pain or pleasure (or a combination of both) to particular experiences and actions, and what you can do to change this—to literally recondition your pain/pleasure connections. How does that sound?

But before we get to that, for now, becoming aware and gaining clarity on what associations *don't* serve you is a very important first step. I would like to share with you some insights that can increase your awareness of what is actually happening to you when you get shut down or take yourself out of the game. Very often awareness alone can be a catalyst for change.

In addition, I will share some specific strategies and techniques you can apply that will help you to direct the focus of your mind, so you can be immersed in behaviors that will support you instead of hurt you.

The first—and what I consider to be absolutely the most important topic to consider is an emotion that has crippled the creative efforts and the success of countless numbers of people throughout history. This one emotion can literally be poison to an otherwise healthy state of mind. It prevents many people from just moving on and taking the actions they need to, and it definitely falls into the **pain** side of the emotional spectrum.

It is also an emotion that, in my opinion, has not received nearly the attention it deserves in the training and coaching community. Now, you may think you know what I am referring to at this point, so I would like to point out that the emotion I am talking about is *not* fear.

Please understand that yes, our fears can be limiting, paralyzing barriers—no question about it. I do a lot of work with my clients, both privately and at public seminars, to assist them in moving beyond the fears and doubts that hold them back. That being understood, addressing fears is something that most competent coaches, trainers, facilitators, therapists and counselors out there today are already *very* aware of and do work on quite frequently.

I wish I had a dollar for every seminar or workshop I've seen that had a line somewhere in its promotional literature saying something like "transform your fears," or, "move beyond your fears." Most people I have met who are committed to personal development and improving themselves are very often aware, at least to *some* degree, of the impact fear is playing in their life.

This in no way downplays the critical importance of having the courage to confront and eventually move beyond your fears—not by any stretch. But there is another emotion that can be just as debilitating, if not *more* so, than fear. An emotion that, if left unchecked, will actually *feed* your fears. It is an emotion that I believe very often goes undetected, just off the radar for most people. The emotion I am referring to is **guilt.**

When I say "guilt," what I mean is the feeling that you don't deserve something or are not worthy of something because you've screwed up or done something wrong in the past—the feeling that you are bad or wrong, or even dirty in some way, because of something you didn't do the way you or someone else thought you should have.

It's a feeling that clings to you and very often taunts you, like a taskmaster or a jailor. It very often keeps you in an endless loop of self-deprecating dialogue with yourself, leaving you unable to move on. It is the epitome of negative self-judgment. To one degree or another, it is a refusal to let go of the past, and this is something that affects *so many* of us.

For example, are you one of those people who makes a mistake and then immediately says to yourself, "Why do I always screw things up!" Or, when you get a bad break or encounter some bad luck, do you ask yourself questions like, "Why do these things always happen to me?" as if it were written somewhere that that's how it is supposed to be.

One question that often comes up in discussing this negative, limiting emotion is "why?" Why do people allow themselves to habitually experience an emotion that is so debilitating? Have you ever felt guilty about something when consciously you know you shouldn't, or when the guilt didn't really make any sense and you found yourself asking the question: "Why do I feel so guilty about this?"

I believe people indulge guilt for several reasons:

1. It is how we're brought up. Many of us are taught from a very early age that if we make a mistake or are not perfect in some way, then we are wrong and we should feel guilty about it. We are taught that feeling guilty is the appropriate response.

2. We believe that if we feel guilty and beat up on ourselves for not getting a certain result or for being a certain way, then that means we are holding ourselves to a "higher standard." We think, "I may not have gotten the result here, but look how guilty I feel about it! That *must* mean that it's important to me." People confuse guilt with impeccability or being driven.

3. Very often, guilt represents a much larger perception or story that we have going on about ourselves and have been carrying with us for years, for who knows what reasons. It is simply a trigger to some larger dialogue, which we have been conducting with ourselves. It can reflect a feeling of not being worthy, a memory of something one of our parents complained about or criticized us for as a child,

or an observation someone made that stuck with us, and so much more.

4. Sometimes our inner voice, also known as "infinite intelligence," "the universe," "our higher self," or whatever you choose to call it, will intuitively tell us in a soft, non-judgmental way that something we are doing is not the right way or the right path. But after receiving that pure impulse, our conscious mind will distort it into negative self-judgment and self-deprecating internal dialogue that takes us down a negative spiral—and *voila!* **Guilt**.

There are many reasons why you may be hanging onto feelings of guilt or shame. Whatever the reasons, the bottom line is *guilt can be crippling!*

HOW TO COUNTERACT THE EFFECTS OF GUILT

So what can we do to counteract the detrimental effects of guilt in our lives?

Well, first we can make a few distinctions that change how we view guilt and what it means to us. For example, realize that *feeling guilty about something does not mean that you have high standards for yourself in that area.* Just because you beat up on yourself for not doing something well, doesn't mean you are committed to excellence.

And in response to the little voice of resistance that may have just come up in your head while reading that, let me respond: ***No it doesn't!*** You're making that up! If you feel guilty about something, do you know what it means? All it means is that you feel guilty. You're no more noble than the person who can take her mistakes in stride and move on.

Let me ask you a question. Do you know—or have you ever known — someone who is *extremely* successful in some or many aspects of life, someone you really look up to, who is generally guilt-free in the way she carries herself *even when she makes mistakes?* She's not always beating up or scolding herself about every little thing. Conversely, do you know anyone who is not particularly successful, at least not by your standards, but who is *constantly* beating up on himself or focusing on what he's doing wrong, or who is constantly immersed in a state of guilt?

If you've been on this earth for any fair amount of time, I would say the chances of your answering "yes" to both of those questions is extremely high. So *guilt, contrary to popular perception, is not what determines greatness or high standards.*

I am not saying that you shouldn't listen to what your conscience tells you is right or wrong in any given situation, or that you shouldn't adhere to the moral compass you've adopted from your parents, your religion, your upbringing, or wherever you got it. That is not for me to tell you and is not the point I'm trying to make here. And I am certainly not saying that you should not push yourself.

What I *am* saying is that you don't have to beat up on yourself to be successful. You don't have to dwell on past mistakes as a license to be able to claim that you hold yourself to a high standard. Does that make sense? Do your best, learn from your mistakes, and *move on!*

To be even more specific, the following are some declarations or statements you can make to yourself to interrupt the patterns of guilt when they begin:

"This confirms it; I'm not perfect. Well, that takes the pressure off."
"You're not perfect! Will you just get that!"
"Okay, so I screwed up. So what? Neeeeeeext!"
"Oh, get over yourself!"
"You are too funny."

It's important to be clear on the tone (out loud, or to yourself) that you are using when you say these types of things to yourself. It's like when you're being tolerant with a little child who keeps making the same mistake. He just can't seem to get it right. You can choose to yell at him and make him feel stupid, or you can choose to be compassionate and understanding and just laugh it off.

Here's one that is incredibly effective, if done with the right tone and intention:

"I forgive myself. It's okay."

This is *very* powerful, because it involves one of the most powerful, cleansing, purifying emotions on the face of the planet: ***Forgiveness.*** This is something I will be talking about more in the last chapter in a very powerful way.

I'd like you to think about something that you've been holding onto, something that has been bothering you and causing you feelings of guilt and embarrassment. Please take a moment to contemplate this.

Please really take that moment.

Notice what comes up for you as you process this in your mind—without getting into a dialogue about what's right or wrong, or what you should have done or not done, etc.—once you've gotten a bearing on it and you're in touch with it, I would simply like you to repeat the following statement with a sense of compassion and true forgiveness. You can say this out loud or to yourself:

"I forgive myself. It's okay."

I would like you to repeat that to yourself, out loud or in silence if you prefer, with all of the sincerity and feelings of forgiveness you can conjure. *And here is the key:* Please do it as if you were forgiving *someone else*, but direct the same level of compassion and forgiveness to yourself instead. It's interesting how often we find it easy to forgive others, but we are much, much harder on ourselves. Give yourself the same latitude you would give another human being.

Please do that for a few moments, or as long as you would like to. Feel free to put this book down as you go through that process.

Think about the topics or issues that came up for you while you were repeating this.

Now, I'm not saying this is necessarily going to solve all of your problems instantaneously. Although if it does, heck, at least be open to that. But can you see how accessing this intention on a consistent basis can help you move on more quickly and not dwell unnecessarily on mistakes or setbacks you might impose upon yourself?

Watch an episode of the television show *Mr. Bean,* or one of the *Mr. Bean* movies with Rowland Atkinson for that matter. This guy can't get anything right! But he lives in a constant state of forgiveness, and you'll notice that one way or another, he always seems to triumph in the end. And I think we all have a little bit of Mr. Bean in us. I know I do.

The next one is critical in getting past the guilt associated with making a mistake or being imperfect: ask yourself the question, **"What can I learn from this?"** I don't say this necessarily from an "everything will be alright in the end" life perspective. I say it from a strategic point of view. You see, when you can take away a lesson or learning experience from a setback, it makes the setback easier to swallow, because you *know* there is a good chance at least that you will be better the next time around and perhaps won't make the same mistake again.

ADDITIONAL MIND MANAGEMENT TOOLS

Here are some other tools you can use to manage your states of mind and emotions in general—and enhance your confidence on a consistent basis.

First of all, remind yourself of the victories and successful experiences you've had in the past. **Ask yourself questions** like:

"What are some truly amazing things I've accomplished in my life?"
"What was the last really big win I had?"
"When was the last time I can remember really being on top of my game? What did that feel like?"

I'm sure if you search your memory banks long enough, you can find *something*. This points to a very important aspect of successfully managing your state of mind, and that is the *quality of the* **questions** you ask yourself. In discussing how to communicate effectively with other people, you will hear me consistently talk about the quality of the questions you are asking to effectively direct the conversation. Well, I have a big question for you: what kinds of questions are you asking *yourself?* Notice that many of the responses I shared above are not statements; they are *questions*. If you direct the questions you ask yourself on a consistent basis, you will direct the focus of your mind.

Next—and this is so powerful—**mental imagery.** This is the act of creating images in your mind. Once again, they can be of past successes or victories, or of future outcomes that you wish to manifest. Get a clear, detailed, mental picture of how that outcome is going to look.

When doing this, I encourage you to be as specific and as detailed as possible. I also want to point out that this is a skill. If you don't think you are particularly good at it, practice, and you will be amazed at how quickly you can become effective at it. Remember these expressions: "A picture is worth a thousand words," and "Seeing is believing." As common as they are, there is a reason why these phrases have been around for so long. It's because visualization is extremely powerful!

Just as powerful as visualization, if not more so, are **declarations.** These are verbal commands you give yourself—internally or out loud—with intensity and heavy repetition. These can take the form of whatever you wish to create or manifest in your life. For example: "I am a powerful closer! I am a powerful closer! I am a powerful closer!" or "Everyone says yes to me! Everyone says yes to me! Everyone says yes to me!"

There are many possible affirmations you can create for yourself.

As I write this book, the movie (and the book) *The Secret* has already been out for quite some time. This movie talks in detail about the "law of attraction" and how your thoughts are frequencies of vibration that are constantly attracting people and circumstances into your life that are of similar vibration.

This principle was already understood and was practiced by many before *The Secret* came out. For those who were paying attention, Napoleon Hill said it rather clearly over seventy years ago in *Think And Grow Rich,* and others before him professed this as well. But *The Secret* put it into a package and presentation that has been rolled out to the mainstream in a way that was never done before. I believe it is absolutely valid when applied properly.

Conventional teaching on this topic states that you must be consistent with your affirmations, that the declarations are most powerful when done with strong positive emotion, and that they must be stated in the positive in relation to what you want, not negating what you don't want. For example, you would want to focus your mind on saying "I will remember!" instead of "I will not forget!" Apparently, infinite intelligence doesn't hear the "not" and would have you forget.

I don't claim to be an expert on this topic and I will confess that I tend to spend most of my energy on being in action and making things happen rather than attempting to "think" my results into reality. But I have noticed that when I am keeping the right kinds of affirmations present in my mind, which often can be easier said than done, positive people and circumstances do tend to show up in my life more consistently. The way it has occurred in some instances has been so uncanny that it left me believing there *had* to be something to it.

And last, but certainly not least, manage your **physiology.** Physiology simply refers to the various ways in which you move and use your body.

Specifically the way you stand, the way you breathe, and the way you move and gesture. Managing the way you move your body can have a huge impact on your states of mind and the way you feel.

You can use what I call *access moves.* I refer to these types of moves in this way because they give you *access* to your power. They give you *access* to focus and to energy. This could be as simple as standing up, stretching out, and taking a few deep breaths if you feel your energy starting to slip—or going for a brisk walk to clear your mind. It could be a ritual of movements you tend to go through before getting into the zone. I still haven't figured out why over 90% of all professional baseball players grab their crotch and spit before stepping into the batter's box, but it seems to work. I don't think that would go over very well in most boardrooms.

Some more extreme examples are getting a cardiovascular workout, going to the gym, or practicing martial arts. Are you going to tell me you wouldn't feel differently after those activities? I'm sure at this point, you've heard of things such as endorphins, and about how exercise changes your biochemistry. That is a real science; be willing to use it. You'd be amazed at how much of an impact managing your physiology can have on your state of mind and emotions. I can also tell you that combining affirmations with an intense cardiovascular workout can be a very powerful experience.

You don't have to understand scientifically how all of that works. Just use it. I'm sure most people don't understand all of the inner workings that occur in a car engine when it starts, but they still stick the key into the ignition to get the car going. *Same thing with your body!* You don't have to understand all of the scientific processes that occur when you use your physiology and practice your access moves—just use them!

DO WHATEVER IT TAKES

By now, you may be noticing that I don't mince words when I write. Simply put: *Whatever it takes, do everything within your power to direct the focus of your mind consistently!*

I believe a quote I recently read from Edith Armstrong sums it up well: "I keep the telephone of my mind open to peace, harmony, health, love and abundance. Then, whenever doubt, anxiety or fear try to call me, they keep getting a busy signal—and they'll soon forget my number."

Manage your mind effectively and the universe will ever so subtly bend to your desires. If you don't, you will always be at the mercy of the circumstances and conditions around you. Commit to doing whatever you have to!

In the next chapter, I am going to talk a bit more about what specifically **determines** what we link to pain and pleasure. When you know this, you can be proactive in reconditioning those connections and create habits and patterns of behavior that support you, set you up to win on a consistent basis, and put you directly on the path to sales mastery and becoming a true sales samurai.

REVIEW:

- The *single most important factor* that separates those who achieve the results they're committed to from those who don't is that the former consistently manage their states of mind and emotion, and they finish what they start.
- When I refer to the mind, I am talking about **that entire experience of *thought, emotion, feeling, memory, intention, self-concept, intellect* and *skill*, that contributes to who you are, how you function and how you experience life.**
- Just like an elephant left to its own devices, the mind can be incredibly destructive and dangerous and inflict great damage. But, properly trained and disciplined, it can achieve massive feats and accomplish incredible results.
- You absolutely want to manage your states of mind because the degree to which you *do not* is the degree to which your follow through and your success are left to chance.
- Ultimately, at the root level, people are driven by two twin forces: the need to avoid *pain* or the desire to gain *pleasure.*
- The problems begin when you associate pleasure to those actions and behaviors that do not serve you, and pain to actions and behaviors that do. This very often occurs on a subconscious level and through repetitive conditioning.
- A great way to uncover disempowering pain/pleasure associations is to observe and take stock of how you behave in relation to taking important action.
- A painful emotion that holds many people back, and which often goes undetected, is *guilt.*

- A great way to positively condition your mind is to notice what you tend to say to yourself when disempowering emotions arise, and then create new responses in their place.
- Questions you ask yourself, mental imagery, declarations, and the effective use of your physiology are all powerful ways to control the focus of your mind.

2

YOUR BELIEFS: THE PAIN/ PLEASURE NAVIGATOR

THE KEYS TO THE KINGDOM

There is an important navigational tool in applying the pain/pleasure principle described in the previous chapter. If you have not yet read that chapter, which I strongly recommend before beginning this one, the principle simply states that ultimately human beings' behavior is dictated by two driving forces: either the need to avoid *pain* or the desire to gain *pleasure.*

Any attempt to apply this principle leads us to one very important and inevitable question: *What determines what we link to pain and what we link to pleasure?* In other words, what directs these twin forces?

The answer to that question, in my experience, is your **beliefs**—your personal belief systems. If you want to talk about an absolutely critical element in designing a successful life, the kind of life that really gets you excited and creates a state of mind that sets you up to win on a consistent basis, that element is your personal belief systems.

*Your personal belief systems will ultimately determine the actions you
take, the way you feel, the potential you tap into, and the results you
create on a consistent basis.*

WHAT IS A BELIEF?

When looking at this critical topic, another inevitable question comes
up: *What is a belief?* Many people have heard the word "belief" used often,
in many different conversations, but few have a true working definition
of this word. In fact, like the mind, a belief is a very simple concept with a
rather broad definition.

According to Webster's, a belief is a, **"conviction that certain
things are true —an opinion, expectation, judgment."** Another
definition I have found very useful is that a belief is nothing more than a
"feeling of certainty about what something is going to mean," (*The Tony
Robbins Personal Power Program.*)

It is the meaning or definition that we designate to a particular topic that
affects how we experience that topic. A belief is also a rule or generalization
we create that determines what has to happen for us to experience a certain
result or feel a certain way. It is the meaning and definition we designate
to the various experiences in our lives—what we think they are going to
mean, and how we think they will make us feel.

You may want to read the previous three paragraphs over again,
because they can truly give dimension and clarity to understanding your
beliefs and what impact they have on your life. But the bottom line is, it
is your beliefs that will ultimately determine what you link both pain and
pleasure to.

THE STRUCTURE OF BELIEFS

Now when you talk about the *structure* of beliefs, basically, there are
two types. One is what I call **Conditional Beliefs**, worded in the form of
"If_____, then_____". For example, "If I win, then I'm worthy," or, "If
I lose, then I'm worthless."

The second type is what I call **Generalized Beliefs**, and these are usually worded in the form of **"Life is_____," "People are_____," "I am_____."** These are more general; for example, "Sales is tough." "Sales is great." "People are kind." "People are cruel."

Very often, generalized beliefs have a reason or rationale attached to them. As a result, they are often either preceded or followed by the word **"because."** So for example, "They won't want to listen to me, *because* people are very close-minded," or, "Of course they'll want to listen to me, *because* generally people want to hear about a great idea."

Some beliefs are interrelated or connected and can be a combination of several beliefs simultaneously, both generalized and conditional; for example, *"If* I don't get the result that I want, *then* I'm a failure; *because* successful people always achieve their intended outcomes."

The conditional belief is: "If I don't get the result that I wanted, then I'm a failure," and the generalized belief (preceded by "because") is: "successful people always achieve their intended outcomes." In this case, a generalized belief is used to substantiate a conditional belief.

Your beliefs ultimately determine the actions you take, the potential you tap into, and the results you generate on a consistent basis.

Yes, that was repeated—intentionally! Because I *really* want you to get this. Your beliefs about yourself—what you're good at, what you're bad at, what you're capable of, and what you deserve—all make up your self-concept. Your beliefs about the outside world, people, places, things, and life all determine how you *experience* that outside world.

In the case of the samurai, some of their beliefs were so strong that they were willing to die for them. And they often did. Their beliefs on dedication and loyalty were such that they would often take on the role of **retainer**, dedicating their entire life to serving another, called simply their **master** or **lord**. The levels of trust and dedication that were displayed in this relationship are seen as extreme by today's standards.

Perhaps an even greater illustration of the sheer depth of samurai belief is evident in the practice known as *seppuku*. To the samurai, suffering public shame or dishonor was unthinkable. This could have been losing in battle, not living up to your Master's expectations, making a crucial mistake, or a host of other examples. And I'm sure the Samurai had a collection of conditional beliefs that defined what warranted shame and what did not.

If put in such a position, the only option for the samurai was death! The global belief that could be described here is: *"An honorable death is more desirable than a life in shame."* The result of this belief was a very particular type of death, where the samurai would gut himself in the stomach with his own short sword.

It was believed that this kind of death would release the spirit most powerfully and efficiently. One of the greatest honors he could bestow upon another samurai was to have that individual chop off his head immediately after the fatal thrust—thus avoiding a long, slow, and extremely painful death. Now *that*, my friend, is a commitment to one's beliefs!

I could just imagine working for a sales organization that operated according to those standards. I'd like to see how those sales meetings ended. And you think getting chewed out by your sales manager is intense?

LIMITING BELIEFS

One of the greatest limitations in life, one of the greatest barriers to human potential, are limiting beliefs—beliefs that hold you back and that keep you from really going for it in life and discovering your *true* greatness.

Now you may be wondering, "Well, Mitch, if beliefs are so important, why do people carry around limiting beliefs in the first place?" Well, think about it: where and how do you acquire your belief systems? Do you handpick each and every one consciously, saying to yourself the entire time, "I choose this belief because it is in my best interests and it will serve me and give me the things I want most out of life"?

No! As a rule, your beliefs are acquired through a lopsided combination of human experience. You get a lot of them in your youth from the people around you—friends, family members, teachers, musicians, athletes, actors—very often when you're too young to even know what's in your best interests to begin with. The media certainly doesn't help either—between television, movies, music, news, videos, videogames, etc.

This is a very inexact science. It's no wonder so many people walk around with so many limiting, debilitating beliefs. By the age of twelve, whether they're playing a role in your life by that time or not, most of us have already acquired enough limiting beliefs to last a lifetime. And unfortunately, in some cases, that's *exactly* what happens—*they last a lifetime!*

So why are limiting beliefs so debilitating?

It's because they can prevent you from taking action when you most need to. They lead you to associate pain with actions that are in your best interests, and pleasure with doing things that do not serve you.

If your definition of prospecting, for example, the beliefs you have around that involve pain and inconvenience, and you focus on the rejection and lack of results instead of on the pride of pushing yourself for a chance to be in the game and for the opportunity to create new contacts and make more money. What do you think you are going to associate to prospecting? *Massive pain!* Those are your beliefs in that area, and they are what determine how you experience that situation.

IDENTIFYING YOUR LIMITING BELIEFS

So, are all of your beliefs setting you up to win and supporting you to take the actions you need to consistently? My answer to that is: probably not.

Think about this: what are some limiting beliefs you have that are holding you back? They can be beliefs about yourself, people, selling, the world around you, life, love, relationships, business, health, money—any beliefs that hold you back, that literally stunt your growth as a human being or as a professional. While this may not be easy, would you agree that this is worth looking at? Would you agree that it might be worthwhile to identify some of the mental and emotional barriers that stand in your way?

If you can do something to improve yourself as a human being, something that will help you to be better at something, why not spend some time on it? I've never heard of anyone who has passed on to the next life with a tombstone that read: "Wished he had watched more television," or "Wished she had spent more time sitting around the house doing nothing." Make sense?

Examples of some limiting *conditional* beliefs would be *"If* someone says no to me or doesn't accept my proposal, *then* I have failed," or *"If* I have been prospecting all day and haven't gotten any results, *then* I'm no good at this."

Examples of some limiting *generalized* beliefs would be "I'm too young," "I'm too old," "I don't have enough education," "I'm the wrong color," "I'm the wrong sex," "You can't trust anyone," "No one wants to hear what I have to say anyway."

Now you may be reading this and saying to yourself, "Well thank you Mitch, that makes a lot of sense and I understand what you mean, but oh no, not me; I don't have any limiting beliefs. I am a *totally self-actualized human being*!"

Well, if that's your opinion, I have a few things to say. First of all, get over yourself! Seriously though, there have been very few—if any—perfect, totally self-actualized human beings without any limiting beliefs to walk this planet. With all due respect, the chances of you being one of them are between slim and none. And you heard about Slim right? He ain't been around for years.

Secondly, you may feel that way not because you're being arrogant, but because you really can't identify the limiting beliefs. You may have a bit of a blind spot in certain areas. You just don't see them.

If that's the case, I encourage you to take a look at some of the areas in your life where perhaps you're not showing up as strongly as you'd like. Where maybe you're not being as consistent and effective as you know you really could be. Where maybe you're not getting the level of results you know you're capable of.

Take a close look. Might there be some limiting beliefs embedded in there somewhere—ones you just didn't notice before—that are playing a role in that area of your life on a consistent basis? For example, do you notice that sometimes, without realizing it, you tend to procrastinate on prospecting or cold-calling or following up on leads because you really don't want to hear the word "*no?*" It's not that you don't do it eventually, but just that you're not doing it as quickly or as often as you could. You may be very clever or subtle in how you're procrastinating, but those habit patterns are showing up nonetheless.

When you think about the reasons behind it, you notice that when you hear that word, when people reject you or shoot you down, it doesn't make you feel all that great. And when you think about why that is (I mean, really think about it), is it because you're still carrying around the feeling, even a little bit, that when someone says "*No,*" to you, it means you've failed, or you aren't good enough, or you really screwed up, or this person doesn't like you, or something like that?

You may have thought you had totally gotten past that one, but it's still kind of hanging around there in the background. I mean, think about it, with so many great things to gain from prospecting aggressively and from following up on leads voraciously, why else wouldn't you do it more powerfully? Remember, sometimes limiting beliefs are subconscious; they exist just off the radar screen of your conscious mind. But they're there, every day, affecting the way you feel, the actions you take, and the results you get.

It's not until you are willing to really take an honest self-inventory, and really take a close look, that they rear their ugly heads. Does that make sense?

A large part of self-mastery, whatever that may look like for you, is developing a set of beliefs that support you and move you in the direction of the behaviors and results you truly desire.

I'll tell you that I have been involved with personal development and what is also known as "transformational" type work for close to twenty years. I have done some very intense work on myself and have taken some very rigorous personal inventories, and—without being arrogant—I feel myself to be further along in that process than the majority of people out there in terms of being able to identify, eliminate, and ultimately replace limiting beliefs that have held me back. Yet I'll be the first to admit that even with someone like myself, there are *still* limiting beliefs that show up in my life from time to time. Because sometimes they are so subtle or so deeply rooted, they're tough to see.

Sometimes, even after you've identified them and they're out in the open, it can *still* take a while to actually address or get rid of them. It doesn't *have* to happen that way, but sometimes it does. Yes, awareness is the first step. But sometimes it takes more than simply awareness.

If you are an experienced veteran of your industry or of sales in general, and you already have a documented track record of proven results, this is intended for *you* in particular.

I say that because the tendency of veterans is to think they already have this handled. Since many of your contacts at this point may be warm market or referrals, the rejection you are confronted with may not be as obvious or overt. I've got news for you. Very often that is *the most intense kind of rejection!*

Because it is coming from someone you already have a longstanding relationship with—not a meaningless stranger. Your procrastination may be more subtle or camouflaged, but it is there—in spades!

The fact is *you must constantly condition your beliefs!* It is a mental muscle, like anything else, and as such it requires consistent upkeep. Imagine if you went to the gym and worked out for a month, got yourself into great shape, and then one day you declared, "Alright, that's it! I'll never have to work out again!" That would be rather foolish.

In the previous chapter, I mentioned that I have reconditioned many of my pain/pleasure connections in a way that truly sets me up for success. One excellent example relates to a limiting belief I used to have in the area of business. When I first got out of college, before I actually got into my current entrepreneurial lifestyle in which sales and marketing play a large role, I used to *believe*: "**The only thing *all salespeople***"—and I grouped them together like they were all one group, this one body of people—**"care about is making money."**

I believed salespeople did not care about the people they sold to, and would do whatever they had to do, say whatever they must, to make a dollar. I believed that if you were in any kind of sales job or were someone who made money on commission, then that was the only thing that mattered to you: money. You were probably a one-dimensional, shallow, materialistic person who didn't really care about anything else. Why would you get into sales unless that was all you cared about?

Unfortunately, to one degree or another (although perhaps not always to such an extreme), this is actually a stereotype and misconception that a lot of people carry around about sales professionals.

And unfortunately, it's also a belief that many sales professionals carry around about *themselves*. Now, do you see how carrying around a belief like that could have held me back from really going for it and thriving in a sales career, or in any entrepreneurial endeavor for that matter? It was a total disconnect!

It's kind of like saying, "I want to be a really great swimmer, but anyone who goes in the water is a slime bag." Imagine a samurai who was loyal to his lord and honored the way of Bushido, but was of the belief that anyone who carries a sword around was a real loser.

When I first made a shift into a career in sales, my first significant brush with it head on was working for an office solutions corporation selling copiers, faxes, and things of the like door to door. Shortly after, I moved into the financial services industry, where I planted myself for close to seven years. For the first few years of my sales career, I really struggled with this belief. It held me back and it definitely affected the quality of my results in a *big* way.

Now keep in mind that at the time, I didn't actually *realize* this. My belief was subtle and deeply rooted. But then I began to explore my beliefs about selling. I remember listening to an audio program called, "The Psychology Of Selling," by Brian Tracy, a phenomenal sales trainer. That was a key moment in my career. I'll never forget it. That program had me take a very close look at my entire perspective on sales and professional selling.

The new belief I created was that *being in sales is actually a noble pursuit.*

If your intentions are honorable and you intend to do the right thing for your client, and *if* you bring a level of expertise, guidance, or information to your client that he would not have had otherwise, *then* there is absolutely nothing wrong with an exchange of value—also known as money for goods or money for services—being rendered.

I'll even go a step further on this and say that the mindset of the modern sales professional epitomizes the entrepreneurial spirit that has made the United States (for example) the powerhouse that it is, and it is why so many other countries, while they like to take pot shots at us from the side, try to emulate the system and success we have created.

Sales is a noble and wonderful thing, and if your job, your life, your business involves selling in any way, shape, or form, it is a true gift. You should be proud of it and embrace it with a passion! The only two conditions you need for that to be your reality are to:

1. Truly believe in both what you are selling and the value it brings to your clients.
2. Operate your business with integrity.

This created a total **paradigm shift** for me in terms of how I viewed professional sales and being a member of that community. I became unstoppable, and my levels of skill, confidence and mastery skyrocketed!

And guess what. What I've outlined here is just *one example* of a limiting belief I identified and overcame. When I created a new, supportive, empowering belief to replace it, I created so much more for myself in terms of potential, possibilities, and bottom-line results. I was freed up to ask for the order and go for the money aggressively and confidently, in a way that is professional and appropriate, when it is the right thing to do.

Right now you may be saying to yourself, "Well, gee, Mitch, that one is easy! I already knew that one." Then I'm glad to say that you're a step ahead compared to where I was back in the day. Let that be a positive omen for your potential (or continued) success in the world of professional sales.

But trust me, you have some limiting beliefs of your own. They just look and sound different. It is amazing when I consider the array of limiting beliefs and personal barriers I have helped some of my consulting clients break through, both individually and as entire organizations. Very often these were barriers I never would have assumed at first glance. Some of the personal transformations have been astounding.

There are many different beliefs we walk around with throughout the course of our lives. Some are supportive and empowering, driving you forward to live a healthy, powerful and profitable life; others are disempowering and limiting, holding you back, stunting your personal growth, and stealing money from you with every breath you take. They are there hovering, orbiting incognito in this thing we call "your mindset." They affect your behavior and the results you are creating every day of your life.

So is there a lot at stake for you regarding this topic? You better believe it!

What are some of your limiting beliefs that have held *you* back?

HOW DO YOU IDENTIFY A BELIEF?

Before you answer the question of what your limiting beliefs are, I have one more important question to ask you. *How do you identify a belief?* As you're reading this, you may be saying to yourself, "Yeah, Mitch, I'm sure I have some limiting beliefs, but I can't seem to identify them. It all seems sort of fuzzy." For someone who is new at this, it can seem a bit daunting. Even for someone who is experienced at this, it's useful—and I would say essential—to review the fundamentals.

Believe it or not, like so many other useful things in life, it's actually rather simple.

Realize first of all that generally, the thoughts you have lead to the emotions you experience. As I once heard said at a seminar that I was attending, "Your thoughts lead to your feelings, your feelings lead to your emotions, your emotions dictate your actions and your actions ultimately determine your results."

To identify your personal beliefs, you simply use words to define an emotional experience.

I'm going to state this in more detail; please read this very closely, because this one skill alone could have a huge impact on the quality of your life.

To identify your personal beliefs, you simply identify the rules, reasons, or definitions you have in your mind that create or bring on a particular emotion(s) you experience habitually. And you put that experience into words.

This may sound a bit general, but allow me to clarify. I mentioned that one of the limiting beliefs I used to have was that, "if someone is in sales, then all they care about is money." So how did I identify that belief?

Well, what I did first was notice that I habitually got unpleasant feelings or emotions when it came time to cold call or go out into the field to make new contacts or create new opportunities. In particular, I would feel nervous or intimidated, or just extremely uninspired. My voice would even tighten up. As I used to say, I would go from a baritone to a soprano in under a minute. I then observed how my mind, consciously or otherwise, was analyzing that situation—what rules, reasons, or definitions it had attached to that particular experience—and I simply *put them into words*.

I'd like you to imagine that putting it into words is the flashlight that sheds light on the actual belief. It takes the intangible and makes it tangible. I noticed that when it came time to cold call, I would feel nervous—not an entirely uncommon experience for anyone who is new to sales. So I would ask myself, "Why am I feeling nervous?"

What I came up with was this: "I feel nervous because I'm calling these people to sell them something, and they know it. And all salespeople care about is money and what they can get from other people and that's how I'm going to be perceived. That's not what I'm about and not what I want to be doing with my life, so why am I doing this? They're going to see right through it anyway."

As you can see, there was quite a bit of disempowering internal dialogue there. You'll also notice that I was able to outline the key, core, limiting belief, **which was:** "All salespeople care about is money and what they can get from other people."

VOILA! I identified a limiting belief!

The best way to identify your limiting beliefs is to observe in what areas you tend to experience negative, limiting emotions or patterns of behavior. For example, if you're in sales, marketing, or some type of entrepreneurial endeavor, do you experience the belief that I just mentioned? Perhaps everything is fine until you have to actually ask for the money, or get your prospect to commit to the transaction. Do you say, **"I don't want them to think I'm selling them,"** like it's a bad thing? Or:

"If I ask them for the money, they'll lose respect for me."

"If I ask them for the money now, they won't like me anymore, and they will probably want to end the conversation."

"Now isn't the right time."

"If I ask for the money, that is probably going to piss them off."

"If I ask them for the money, they'll write me off as just another salesperson."

"If I ask for the money, they'll think I don't care about the relationship and that all I really care about is the money."

"Asking for the money means I'm being pushy."

Or how about this: Do you feel embarrassed or nervous when you have to ask for help, or when you have to delegate to others? Do you say to yourself things like:

"Well, if I have to ask for help, then I must be doing something wrong."

Or:

"I can't do it myself, and that certainly isn't acceptable."

Let's look at it on a broader scale. Do you tend to tense up when it comes to approaching someone romantically and expressing how you feel? Or do you not trust members of the opposite sex? Do you not trust members of your own sex? Do you shudder at the thought of public speaking? Do you seem to avoid commitment like the plague?

Are there certain things you're not even willing to attempt because you feel as if you've already been down that road and been beaten by it? I'd like to give you a brief exercise to really get clear about this. You might be amazed at how enlightening this is.

I'd like you to take what I have been covering here and identify some *limiting beliefs* that have held you back. I encourage you to focus more specifically on areas of business. If you are in a sales or entrepreneurial related position, focus even more specifically on beliefs related to those activities. This is what I suggest, but it can be another area if you prefer. Let this exercise be what you want it to be for *you*.

I ask you to focus on the limiting beliefs because we are going to come up with new, supportive, and empowering beliefs to replace them. You obviously want to maintain any supportive empowering beliefs you already have. For the purpose of this exercise, we're not as concerned with identifying those beliefs as we are with identifying the limiting, disempowering beliefs that have held you back. So:

Please consider an area or areas where you are not operating as effectively as you would like to be.

Notice how you are habitually classifying, defining, or generalizing particular aspects of that process in a way that isn't serving you—either in the way you act or in the way you feel.

Then, identify and write down the limiting beliefs that come to mind, using the process I have described above. Put words to the experience.

I encourage you to use a separate piece of paper or workspace for this.

Please do not return to the reading until you have identified at least three limiting beliefs.

Please do that now.

Now, a question: Do the beliefs you've identified serve you in your life and set you up to experience the types of results and emotions you want most on a consistent basis? I bet the answer to that, at least for most of the beliefs you've identified, is, *"no!"*

Think about that. You have been carrying these beliefs around for who knows how long!

What's the price?

What has been the cost to you up to this point? What have you been depriving yourself of, leaving on the table, or missing as a result of these limiting beliefs? This could be in financial terms or in other ways as well.

For example, are these beliefs affecting your levels of happiness and satisfaction? Are they affecting your relationships or ability to connect with others? Are they preventing you from taking action or following through more consistently? Are they stealing money from you?

Please take a few minutes or more to write down answers to the questions in the paragraph above: what have been the costs?

Is there a lot at stake here?

Are you motivated to get rid of those beliefs? Would it serve you to eliminate them once and for all? If the answer for you is not a resounding *"Yes!"* I encourage you to look a little deeper.

As you may have read in the introduction of this book, in addition to writing books and creating audio products, I am a consultant, executive coach and seminar leader. I conduct tele-courses, webinars, live seminars, and training events. In my live programs, I actually walk participants through a much more involved and much more emotional process that gets them to really focus on the price they've paid as a result of their limiting beliefs—what the cost has been in *all areas of their life*, not just business.

Of course, with so much pain attached to the costs of carrying around these limiting beliefs, I often get participants who turn that around and go to a place of renewed possibility regarding what they can create for themselves. Very often, they create new beliefs for themselves right there on the spot!

Unfortunately, in this book I don't have the luxury of walking you through that process in person. I do however go through it in the audio program. If you don't have that, I highly recommend you pick it up. But the main goal here is for you to simply *make the distinction, become aware, and see firsthand just how costly these limiting beliefs are.* That alone can dissolve the limiting belief, and it creates a wide-open space to insert a new, supportive, empowering belief. And that is exactly what I would like you to do.

CREATING SUPPORTIVE BELIEFS THAT SERVE YOU

Doubt kills the warrior.
—JUSTIN STERLING

What I'd like you to do now is to create some new, supportive, empowering beliefs to replace the old, negative, limiting beliefs. How do you do that? Simple. **You create an alternative belief that negates the limiting belief.**

You take a look at the same experience and create a different belief! The antithesis of the old belief, if you will. For example, in the case of the belief I mentioned before, the original limiting belief was: "If someone is in sales, then all they care about is money."

The new belief I created was:

"While there are some sales professionals out there who don't care about their clients, there are many sales professionals who care deeply about their clients and who want to protect them and guard their interests. And I am one of them."

Notice I replaced a conditional belief with a generalized belief. You can do that also. Another new belief I crafted was:

"If someone has their clients' best interests in mind and provides a valuable product or service, then there is nothing wrong with an exchange of value—also known as money for goods or money for services—taking place."

Which kind of belief is that? Exactly: another *conditional* belief, because it is worded in terms of "If____, then__."

A very important component of creating new, supportive, empowering beliefs is to create beliefs that the mind can *accept* and really sink its teeth into— beliefs that make sense, as opposed to fluff or just wishful thinking. For example, if the supposed new, empowering belief was: "If someone is in sales, they can be trusted, because everyone is trustworthy and you just shouldn't worry about that kind of thing," well, that's a very nice thought, but my mind would have said "B.S.!" because it just isn't true. Instead, my new belief, which I stated above, was one my mind could really connect with.

There are people out there in the world right now who are living according to old, antiquated, limiting beliefs every day that stop them cold. Are you one of them? Are you open to creating some new beliefs that will move your life in the direction you want it to go?

Please create and write down some new, supportive, empowering beliefs that your mind can accept. Be sure to use the above criteria I have laid out for you as a guide.

To support you in doing this and to make it easier for you, I have given some examples of both limiting and empowering generalized beliefs, as well as limiting and empowering conditional beliefs:

Limiting Generalized Beliefs:

- *Sales is difficult.*
- *You can't trust people.*
- *Money is one big headache.*
- *This market is impossible.*
- *I am too old.*
- *I am too young.*
- *Life's a bitch and then you die.*
- *All salespeople care about is money.*
- *Sales resistance is a bad thing.*
- *Hearing the word "no" is a bad thing.*
- *Challenging someone's opinion is rude.*
- *Asking for referrals is inappropriate.*
- *I must have done_____before I have earned the right to ask for referrals/business/money.*

Empowering Generalized Beliefs:

- *Sales is fun.*
- *People are generally trustworthy.*
- *Money is an amazing tool.*
- *This market will allow me to bring out my best.*
- *There is plenty of opportunity in any market.*
- *Successful people will do well in a slow market, and unsuccessful people will do poorly in a strong market.*
- *Age is maturity and wisdom.*
- *Youth is energy and power.*
- *Life is the most amazing gift.*
- *There are many well-rounded sales professionals, and I am one of them.*
- *There are many sales professionals who do the right thing and care deeply about their clients, and I am one of them.*
- *Sales resistance is a golden opportunity to create a transaction.*
- *If done respectfully and as a good listener, challenging someone's opinion is one of the greatest gifts you can give him or her.*

- *Some of the biggest breakthroughs in my life have come after someone was willing to respectfully challenge my opinion.*
- *Of course I will ask my clients for referrals. It is part of my job. They'd be disappointed if I didn't.*
- *The past d*oes not have to determine my future.

Limiting Conditional Beliefs:

- *If you're in sales, then you're going to have a difficult time.*
- *If you're in sales, then all you care about is money.*
- *If someone says "no" to me, then that is a problem.*
- *If I challenge someone's opinion, then I am being rude.*
- *If I don't get the result, then I have failed.*
- *If it's not perfect, then I have to start all over again.*
- *If I screw up, then I am a failure.*
- *If I don't get the result I want, then I have failed.*
- *If I make the same mistake more than once, I am an idiot.*
- *If it takes longer than _____ to be successful, then it's not going to happen.*
- *If I don't get the result by _____, then it's not going to happen.*

Empowering Conditional Beliefs:

- If *you're in sales, then you can learn and improve by being challenged.*
- *If you're in sales, then you're in a position to help and provide people with solutions.*
- *If someone says "no" to me, then I'm right where I want to be, because this person is telling me how he/she really feels.*
- *If someone says "no" to me, I have some tremendous opportunities in that conversation.*
- *If someone says "no" to me, now I get to learn what's really going on in his or her head.*
- *If I respectfully challenge someone's opinion, I am offering him/her an opportunity to see things differently.*

- *If I don't get the result, it is not a failure, only an outcome. What can I learn from this?*
- *If I screw up, that's okay because it happens to the best of them.*
- *If it's not perfect, I will move forward regardless, because I am not interested in perfection, I am interested in getting the result.*
- *If I make the same mistake more than once, I am more interested in learning from it than beating* up on myself.

Now, there is a very important distinction I want to make here: I am not interested in what is the most accurate belief or what is the absolute truth. I'll leave that one for the philosophers and politicians. I am interested in the beliefs that will be the most **supportive and empowering** to you in a way that does not harm others. When the doctors tell a "terminal" patient that he has another six months to live and the patient goes on to live for another twenty years, does it really matter how accurate or true the doctor's beliefs were?

I hope some of the examples above helped you or at least gave you a clearer understanding of how this process works. What are some new beliefs you created? Do you notice any differences? Do you see how operating with these new beliefs can improve your states of mind and emotion, and the quality of your life? Do you see how they can improve your follow-through and consistency and the results you create? Do you have a goal partner, or a mastermind or a business coach whom you can bounce these off?

Please review them. More importantly, I encourage you to take these new beliefs and *apply them*! That's the key. As a matter of fact, I encourage you to review this as often as you feel necessary to really integrate this.

Keep the dialogue going. If you've had some breakthroughs with this exercise or you now see the importance of cultivating a more empowering crop of belief systems and would like to integrate them, contact my organization and find out what is involved in working with your own personal coach or, as I stated above, having me come out to your organization. Or have someone else out. The point is, do something with this!

Do what you have to do—write down the new, supportive, empowering beliefs you've created and put them in a place where you can see them *consistently*. Recite and repeat them to yourself until your mind becomes familiar with them and integrates them into a way of being. The thing that separates the master samurai from an educated intellectual is she takes her knowledge and puts it into practice. Engage in an ongoing dialogue with yourself internally, or with others out loud, about the validity and usefulness of these beliefs in your life. Make them real!

THE "MIRACLE MAN"

A very inspiring example of the sheer power of your beliefs is a gentleman by the name of Morris Goodman, also known as "The Miracle Man." Mr. Goodman's story is so incredible that it was profiled in the movie called *The Secret*. If you have not yet seen the movie or read the book, I *highly* recommend them.

Mr. Goodman's life is a true example of the sheer, unlimited power of belief if ever I've heard one. Mr. Goodman had the good fortune of experiencing something that very few people ever experience. And I say "good fortune" rather loosely: he was in a plane crash.

Just consider that for a moment. Even more rare than that experience was the fact that he lived to tell about it. Now notice, I didn't say he walked away from it—because he did not. When he arrived at the hospital, he was completely paralyzed. His spinal cord was crushed. He had broken his first and second cervical vertebrate. His swallowing reflex was destroyed. He couldn't eat or drink. He had to be fed intravenously and oh, by the way, his diaphragm was destroyed also. He couldn't even breathe without the help of a respirator. All he could do was blink his eyes.

The doctor told him that he'd be a vegetable for the rest of his life.

That's the picture the "experts" saw of him. But as far as Mr. Goodman was concerned, it didn't matter what they thought. What mattered was what *he* thought and what *he believed*. Not only did he say that he would be able to function on his own and walk again, he made a public commitment to be walking and to be out of the hospital by *that Christmas*.

Why? *Because he believed it was possible.* Of course, the entire staff was shocked when he made that commitment. It seemed not only virtually impossible, but *flat out* impossible.

Mr. Goodman then proceeded to engage in a regimen of breathing, swallowing, and mind-conditioning exercises, the intensity of which I can only imagine. Progress was slow and difficult to say the least and I cannot fathom some of the barriers and emotional tests he was confronted with during that period of time. But guess what: true to his word, he *walked out of the hospital on his own*—by Christmas. Now he lives an active life, full of possibility and experience. He is now, of all things, a professional speaker, amongst other pursuits. He's having a blast, and he is an inspiration to people all over the globe!

The power of belief.

So I have a question: if Morris Goodman can come back from that adversity to be one of the most inspiring examples of possibility and human potential you'll ever hear about—simply through the power of *belief*—is it safe to say that maybe you can spend a little more time each day reaching out to new prospects? Can you get into the office a bit earlier, read the books that will help you master your craft, practice the skills you need to be great at what you do?

I mean, come on!

Can you make a concerted and ongoing effort to identify those beliefs that do not serve you and to develop new, supportive, empowering beliefs that will drive you forward to accomplish what you want out of this life? I certainly hope so.

CONCLUSION

Considering the central role that belief systems play in regards to your self-concept, what you are capable of, and your perception of the world, would it serve you to make upgrading the quality of your beliefs a consistent focus in your life? Of course it would. Make this a part of who you are and watch how your entire life transforms!

REVIEW:

- A belief is a feeling of certainty about what something is going to mean.
- Your personal beliefs determine what you link to pain and what you link to pleasure.
- Your personal belief systems will ultimately determine the actions you take, the way you feel, the potential you tap into, and the results you create on a consistent basis.
- There are two types of basic beliefs: conditional beliefs, worded in the form of "If_____, then_____"; and generalized beliefs, worded in the form of "Life is_____," or "People are_____", for example.
- One of the greatest limitations to human potential is *limiting beliefs*.
- Many sales professionals have limiting beliefs about what it means to be in sales, and this holds them back.
- The great news is that limiting beliefs can be identified, eliminated, and replaced with new, supportive, empowering beliefs. It simply takes work.
- You identify beliefs by observing emotional patterns and using words to describe how your mind is interpreting the world around you to create those patterns.
- The best way to identify *any* beliefs you have–limiting, supportive, or otherwise–is to literally write them down.
- The key to creating supportive, empowering beliefs is to create beliefs that the mind can accept as reality and truly "believe" in–not hype or fluff.
- Once you have clearly identified and articulated beliefs that support you and that the mind can accept, you must do everything within your power to integrate them and make them a part of who you are.

3

GRAB YOUR PROSPECT'S ATTENTION: IDENTIFYING THE BARRIER

IT'S TIME TO STARTLE YOUR PROSPECT!

When looking to get better at something or to experience breakthroughs in a particular area, it is helpful and sometimes necessary to take a look at what the *barriers* are, or what might be standing in your way.

Why is that?

It's because you now have a chance to see what you are dealing with. It helps you get clear on what you need to change, improve, or overcome; it lets you know what has been holding you back. Let me give you an incredibly simple example: If you are walking down the street and there is a cement wall standing in your way, halting your progress, would it not serve you to be able to see and identify the wall so you can make an adjustment and move around or over it? Of course!

Would you also agree that sometimes just being clear on the barrier alone could make all the difference in the world?

I remember, for example, my perception of a great salesman used to be that he was someone who dazzled his prospects with amazing verbal

49

agility. He just took control of the conversation and talked his prospects into handing over the business. He ran verbal circles around them until they didn't know left from right, north from south, and they finally just "submitted."

I really thought that was how it worked and that was my barrier. My *misperception* of salesmanship was literally holding me back from greatness in sales. If you are new to your respective industry, you might be making the same mistake I did. If that is the case, I understand where you are coming from, and you *definitely* need to read on!

When I clearly identified this approach as a barrier and began to instead put my focus towards being a great *listener* and asking effective *questions*, that was when I really stepped up my game as a closer. My success came when I started looking for buying signals and shifts in energy, or for certain questions from the prospect, as opposed to where I could just put my two cents in and sound intelligent.

Another personal example that comes to mind is when I was younger and suffering from chronic stomach problems. Not knowing what was wrong, and worried that I might have a serious illness, I finally went to the doctor and got checked out. It turned out I was simply lactose intolerant. By changing my diet or taking a couple of pills whenever I consumed dairy, I no longer had to worry about it. It may seem like a little thing, but believe me, that made a *huge* difference to my well-being, physical health, and peace of mind. *Just by identifying the barrier or issue.*

Is this making sense?

I would like you to think of some times in your life when, by simply identifying the obstacle(s) holding you back, you managed to have a breakthrough. I encourage you to really do this—not just nod in agreement as you read. And have fun with it! Think about it: Is this not a great subject to focus on—filling your mind with times in your life where you created solutions, breakthroughs, and results simply by understanding what you were up against or what was holding you back? If nothing else, allow this to be an acknowledgment to yourself.

Please write down as many examples as you can think of.

With the above examples firmly in your grasp we can bring it back to the topic of this chapter:

What is the primary barrier to effective interpersonal communication?

Why do I focus on the topic of interpersonal communication in particular?

It is because mastering your interpersonal communication is the basis—the foundation—for attaining true sales mastery. It is the stuff sales is made of. It is tantamount to the samurai understanding that he first had to master the way of the sword before he could even consider calling himself a true samurai.

So is this an important question to have an answer for? Of course! Think about it. What is the primary barrier to effective interpersonal communication? Is it your:

Tone?
Grammar?
Word choice?
Body language?
Volume?
Pace of speech?

I would say all of these things affect communication to one degree or another. But if you want to talk about the main, predominant barrier to effective interpersonal communication and thus success in sales, it is simply this:

As an overwhelming rule, people do not listen!

That's it!

Simple? Yes. Applied effectively in most selling situations? Absolutely not!

I'll prove it.

What are some of the primary complaints people usually have when they feel someone isn't doing a good job of communicating with them?

From close to two decades of experience in the field, and from analyzing human behavior at a very deep level, I have found that some of the predominant complaints are the following:

"I don't feel like you're hearing me."

"I don't feel like you really understand what I'm saying here."

"It's like we're speaking two different languages."

"Hello? Did you hear what I just said?"

"I felt like we had nothing in common."

In business-to-business sales, this is a big one: "We don't really think he/she understands the needs and concerns of our organization."

And this happens on both ends—the person doing the communicating, as well as the person being communicated to. Most of the time, we're just too caught up in our own internal dialogue. I call it "Mental Wax Paper." It distorts our ability to see and hear clearly. This characteristic is all too pervasive in many sales professionals.

So the inevitable question becomes: *How do you become a better listener?*

Well, as regards *our* side of the communication, or in other words, those things that *we* can control, there are several answers to that. We can:

1. **Ask a lot of questions.**
2. **Constantly check in.** Don't be afraid to do it. "Does that make sense?" "Are you with me?" "Do you follow?" You may notice I do that occasionally throughout this book, and anyone who has been to one of my live events knows I do this often.
3. Take on the identity of an **investigative consultant**—be more interested in what you can *learn* versus what you can teach. If you are the expert, it will come through. And if you're not, use that as a *strength*, not a weakness. Point to your firm's track record or resources, or one (or several) of your associates' experience and reputation.
4. **Do not interrupt the prospect's answers.** Let her finish her thoughts and ideas in their *entirety*—not just when you feel it's been enough. Very often, it's at the end of an idea or sentence that you

will get the real meat or intention of what someone is attempting to say and they will reveal their true feelings to you. Learn to notice the subtleties.

5. **Lose this infatuation you have with the sound of your own voice.** You should be hearing your prospect's voice more than your own in the conversation. If that is not the case, then it is very simple: *You are talking too much!* Remember to ask yourself the question: "Whose answers am I more interested in? Hers or my own?" Over time, you develop a sensory awareness of this, where intuitively you are aware of who is doing more of the talking. Be very sensitive to this.

All of the above are important—no question. But would you like to know what I have found to be the *biggest* single adjustment you can make to be a better listener? This is vitally important:

Do not take everything at face value! Do not immediately accept everything the person is saying simply because they're saying it!

Look beyond the surface level meaning of what they're saying to get to their true feelings, or their true state of affairs on the matter.

Let me give you some examples of how this applies. If for example you're in real estate and you're speaking with someone whom you know to be a high net worth prospect, and they tell you that they haven't been looking at a lot of properties recently, or they feel that they are in no rush to make a move or invest, it probably means that they're not a very good prospect—that you would probably be better off investing your time elsewhere, or it's time to move on. Correct?

No! It doesn't necessarily mean that at all. What does it mean if they say they have not been looking at properties aggressively as of late? All it means is that they have not been looking at properties aggressively as of late. For all you know, they could have not found the agent they really trust or feel comfortable with yet. Or they may not have spoken with an individual who created the urgency or got them to see why it was in their better interests to begin exploring different options.

Maybe a few months earlier they made the rounds, didn't see anything they liked, became discouraged and decided, "You know, maybe now isn't the right time." And all it would take is an agent with the right inventory and level of conviction to have them open to the idea again. You just don't know.

Don't accept the initial concern at face value. How would it feel drifting right past someone like that and then finding out another agent put them into a seven figure property months later, simply because you didn't have the conviction or openness to hang in there with them, ask more detailed questions and even challenge them a bit? Don't assume that you always know what it means when someone says something. Don't accept everything they say, just because they say it.

And I'm not saying that everyone is lying to you. I'm saying that they may believe they feel a certain way, until convinced otherwise.

Now that's real estate. Let's take a very different example. Let's say you're in the financial services industry. Let's say you're dealing with someone whom you know to be a high net worth individual, who says he hasn't put any new money into his equities portfolio over the last year.

This assumes of course that you're familiar with his risk tolerance and overall financial objectives, and you know a higher concentration of stocks would be a suitable recommendation. In other words, let's say the basics have already been handled.

But he hasn't put any new money into that portion of his portfolio for the last year. Well, that means that he probably is not a good candidate for new money or a capital infusion into equities. Correct?

No! Once again, if he hasn't put any new money in recently, what does it mean? All it means is that he hasn't put any new money into his equities portfolio as of late.

Maybe he was burned with a stock. Maybe he was approached by financial advisors who did a bad job, weren't listening, or came across with the wrong kinds of ideas. Maybe he read something in a research report or newspaper article that turned him off. Maybe he thinks he has to know more than he really does before making a move that an expert advisor could handle for him.

You just don't know. So don't accept it simply at face value.

Maybe there are other aspects of his overall portfolio that no one has bothered to ask him about. Maybe he's feeling overwhelmed by some tax issues or estate planning. You just don't know unless you investigate properly.

Don't accept defeat or that there are no possibilities to be created here, simply because he hasn't been active as of late. A true Samurai of Sales asks the important questions to get a lay of the land and what is really true for the prospect or client. As far as how to do that, what questions to ask, etc., read on.

The point is, you just don't know so don't take things simply at face value and accept whatever this person is saying to you simply because they're saying it.

Sometimes when someone says, "Now is not a good time," what they're really saying is, "I've had a bad experience before and I'm hesitant to trust someone else," or "I'm hesitant to even discuss this." Or when they say, "It's out of my budget," what they're really saying is, "I just don't feel comfortable yet," or, "I need to know some more about this before I move ahead," or, "Of course I have the money, you just have to get me excited about this."

And let me ask you something. Do you have any idea how powerful it is when you can persuade someone to do business a certain way for the first time in their life or to revisit something they haven't done for years because they didn't feel comfortable doing it with anyone other than you? When you can become their confidant or agent of change in that area? Do you realize how much leverage, and let me just say it—*control*—you now have with that individual?

Also, do you realize how powerful it is to be able to persuade someone to do business with you period, under any circumstance, when they expressed initial concerns or objections that you simply didn't take at face value and you persisted through? It just feels great to know you were able to do that and that you'll be helping this person in a big way moving forward, all because you didn't accept things at face value.

Now, I want to clarify that I'm not saying in doing this you should chase prospects that have no potential, or if someone makes it absolutely clear that they don't want to work with you or do business a certain way, or that something is inappropriate for them, that you should beat a dead horse. I'm not saying that.

The point here is simply not to accept what your prospect is saying just because she's saying it. Don't take things at face value without inquiring, asking and even challenging. That's what being a great listener really is and that's one of the key building blocks to sales mastery.

And if that helps you with your conviction around handling objections and being persistent, then perfect. Because being a great salesperson should be motivation enough. But being a great listener, someone who really gets to the heart of the matter, is a noble and considerate thing to do, whatever your livelihood may be. Does that make sense?

Remember, without looking into the situation a bit more closely, you run the risk of missing tremendous opportunities that others might uncover, that could be found right under your nose simply by inquiring more deeply and being a good listener.

Your goal is to be an "investigative consultant" and an "objective listener." Once again, an "investigative consultant" and an "objective listener." In other words, ask questions skillfully, listen closely and be willing to challenge when appropriate, which you'll find is almost always. This is one of the things that truly separates a sales samurai from the majority of the population.

So that is how to address your own internal dialogue and the barriers to being a great listener. As you can see, my approach here is not to simply give you a bunch of "techniques." That will only get you so far. My approach instead is to create a state of mind and a way of thinking that open you up to becoming a master communicator.

If a budding samurai was only given a handful of unrelated sword moves by his master and no more, he would never master the way of the sword. It is in learning and developing an understanding of the technique as a unified system that he gains true mastery. That is why the subtitle of this book is "*The Path to True Sales Mastery.*" Whatever your current level of success or experience may be, when you commit to this approach, I promise you the rewards and benefits are priceless.

This is critical, because until you do that you will forever be hindered in your communication. But let's say you've handled that. Let's say you are the best listener on the planet.

> "*To give a person an opinion one must first judge well whether that person is of the disposition to receive it or not.*"
> —HAGAKURE, *THE BOOK OF THE SAMURAI*

Then the question becomes, how do you handle it when the *other* person, a.k.a. the prospect, isn't really listening to *you*? Would you agree that having the attention of whomever you're speaking with is just as important? When someone isn't listening to you, it can be especially challenging. You can't know what's going on for them internally—at least not initially.

Why is getting someone's attention so critical? Because until you really have someone's attention, until they're listening to you, most of what you say is going in one ear and out the other. And what they do listen to won't be received with the interest and focus it deserves.

Is that how you want to go through life—not being heard the way you ought to be? Of course not!

Think about what is going on in the mind of your prospect when you are speaking with him. *You believe* he is totally in tune and connected to what you are saying, simply because you are speaking. Not necessarily true! As a matter of fact, it's usually not the case.

First of all, you have to deal with any judgments he may have about you. It could be something about the way you look, sound, or present yourself.

Something about you could remind him of someone he knows or an experience he once had that does not conjure up pleasant memories. You don't know. He could also have skepticism about people in your industry or about sales professionals in general.

In addition, he could simply be caught up in his own thoughts. Maybe he's thinking about an errand he has to run that day, an issue with one of his children, an argument he had with his significant other, or a problem he's having at the office. Who knows?

You won't know if that is the case. Sometimes, when people are tuning out, they make it obvious by de-focusing their eyes or through a dull tone of voice. But sometimes they don't.

With all of this going on in the mind of your prospect, how do you grab her attention?

First and foremost: ***Do not underestimate the power of using someone's first name!***

If you want a classic example of one of the most overlooked tools in the world of professional sales, this is it right here. It is so simple and so powerful, yet so often neglected. The use of someone's name is incredibly powerful. That is because someone's name, especially his or her first name, is what we call a "trigger" sound—it immediately triggers someone's attention.

The sound of someone's name is one of the greatest triggers you can use. Why? Because we've been hearing it our entire life. There is no sound that is more personal or more meaningful. It refers to us directly. It is both *to* us and *about* us.

It is essentially one of the first sounds that we repeatedly hear as children. And it is also the sound our parents or guardians used to control our behavior or get our attention. It is undoubtedly a sound that we connect a lot of emotion and meaning to.

Let me ask you a question. Even as a grown adult, aren't there certain people who can say your name a certain way—whether it's your significant other, childhood friend, family member, whomever—and it *still* has a very real impact on you? That can be positive *or* negative. I know that at times, when my mother would say my name or call out to me, it would remind me of when I was a kid.

Think about how personal the sound of your own name is! Think about how you respond when someone says your name, especially when it is said emphatically. For a split second, it puts you in a brief trance. You feel compelled to turn in their direction, or at least respond with a, "Yes?" or a, "What?"

Very often, that reaction is knee jerk. It just happens. It's rather amazing when you think about it. **Yet it is astounding how many sales professionals do not use their prospects' names to grab attention and create interest.**

When initiating dialogue with your prospect, what is the first thing you want to say? Exactly: *their name.* Don't take their name for granted. Don't sandwich it in between sentences. Let it be the first thing you say, and say it emphatically, as if you have something meaningful to discuss—because you do!

That is why you are contacting them in the first place. If you don't have something meaningful to discuss when you are contacting your prospects, I strongly recommend that you, as a sales professional, reassess that.

Because without that in place, good luck!

Saying their name with an aura of familiarity, as if you already know them, can be extremely effective as well. It makes your prospect immediately say to him or herself, "Do I know this person?" or "Who is this?" There is nothing in the world like infusing your prospect with curiosity.

"John!"

"Lisa!"

"Steve!"

"Marco!"

"Susan!" Etc ...

It is important to make sure you pause after you say their name, to give them an opportunity to respond with a, "Yes?" or, "What?" If you do not give them an opportunity to respond, you may counteract much of the power of using their name, because you aren't giving it an opportunity to sink in and you aren't bringing your prospect into the conversation.

Yes, it's simple. *But make sure you do it!* This alone can drastically alter the receptivity of anyone you speak with within the first five seconds, be it on a personal or professional level, face-to-face or over the telephone. If you were in front of me right now, I might have to scream your name out loud, just to make sure you were listening to this!

BUILDING RAPPORT

I'd like to speak briefly about rapport building. This can take anywhere from fifteen seconds to several minutes to years, depending on the tone and the quality of the relationship. Some would say it never truly ends.

The key here is simply to ask questions and be genuinely interested. If you're not interested, what do you do? Act as if you are! Anyone who is reading this and is married will probably understand exactly what I am talking about.

Seriously, there is no magic bullet here. You must do your best to be— or at least appear to be—genuinely interested in what your prospect has to say and who they are as a human being. If you find you have no interest in any of that, once again, I strongly encourage you to take a look at where you are coming from as a professional and your reasons for being in the business that you are.

Are you coming from a place of service or selfish? If all you care about is closing a sale and making money, eventually your clients will pick up on this, and it could be a major block to building your business or relationships to the level you truly desire.

As long as they are legitimate and you do not lie, there is nothing wrong with planning stories or anecdotes to discuss with prospects in advance. I encourage you to work on your conversation, joke-telling or storytelling skills if you don't feel strong in these areas. You are not being any less "real" or authentic if you prepare in advance to be a good conversationalist.

For example, when someone asks you how you are doing, be prepared to have something interesting to say. When I'm on the phone and reaching out to prospects for the first time, whether they are cold calls or through referral, I have some simple answers I give repeatedly. They are commonplace to me at this point because I have been using them for years, but they are unique and entertaining to the prospect hearing them for the very first time over the phone, from someone they do not yet know. For example:

Me: Hello, [prospect's name]?

Prospect: Yes?

Me: Mitch Harris, aka, "The Samurai Of Sales." How are you doing today?

Prospect: Fine. How about yourself?

Me: Well, if I was doing any better, I think someone would have to write an article about me.

If I was doing any better, I would have to be twins.

Well, I'll tell you [prospect's name], life is good and it's getting even better.

I'll tell you [prospect's name], if you had any idea! Life is good.

I'll tell you [prospect's name], there is some heavy gratitude going on over here.

I understand these answers may seem a bit outside of the box and you may not think they are your "style." But realize there is a big difference between reading it in the printed word and using it as a quick segue when starting a conversation. And these don't need to be your replies per se.

But guess what: if you're calling someone over the phone, a decision-maker who is busy, who gets called often, you *need* to have something that will immediately separate you from the ten other sales calls she is going to get that week! One brief chuckle or something that is a bit different could be all it takes to keep her on the phone and listening. If none of the above responses work for you, I encourage you to create some that do. The point here is to **be different!**

Next, I have a question:

With the mental wax paper that you need to break through in the mind of your prospect and with all of the other considerations—skepticism, his constantly getting contacted by competitors, everyone claiming to have the answer, everyone asking this person for his time, attention, money, trust, etc.—what do you have to do to break through and immediately distinguish yourself from the competition?

You must make a **bold claim** or ask a **bold question.**

You must be willing to appropriately **startle** your prospect. Be dramatic. "Traditional" sales trainers and communication coaches have always said, "You must be able to describe, in several concise sentences, the main benefit you bring to the table and your unique selling proposition, and your identity in the market place and... etc... etc... blah, blah, blah."

This is valid. But the problem is that it's *outdated.* If that's all you're doing, it's not enough. Why is that? *Because nowadays, everyone is already doing that!* Do you prefer a study in how things used to be, or how they are *now*? *Startling people*, as long as it is appropriate and relevant to the conversation or to what they really want, is extremely effective.

Think about it. The most effective marketers on the planet use this strategy constantly, both verbally and visually.

Think about how many television commercials or magazine advertisements you've seen that startle you up front simply to get your attention. I recently saw a computer commercial that showed people dropping and breaking their laptops or spilling coffee on their computers in slow motion to draw your attention to how durable their computers were. Trust me, it got my attention!

Another commercial I saw started out featuring the actor Jimmy Smitts saying, *"Thousands of children all over the city are armed at this very moment!"* It turned out he was talking about how they were armed with education and tools for learning, but it was a great hook and it really got the viewers' attention.

Movie trailers in the theater or upcoming attractions on television always show the most shocking, startling parts of the movies and shows when advertising them. Sometimes the result is that the performance itself is a colossal let down, but the advertisements did a great job of promoting it, simply because they were startling.

Perhaps the greatest example of this is television news promoting future broadcasts. I wish I had a dollar for every time I've heard, "Tonight at 11:00, shocking new footage of ..."—usually followed by news of something truly startling or disturbing. Unfortunately, it's also usually something violent or anti- social. Nevertheless, it is startling, and it does get the attention of the viewer.

I'm sure you've heard the expression, "If it bleeds, it leads." The media doesn't do this because they're evil (although some would disagree with that); they do this because it is effective and it works! If telling viewers that the broadcast at 11:00 was going to have a close-up of grass growing for ten minutes and the ratings were off the charts, I guarantee you more news networks would be providing close-ups of grass. But we know that would not work because it is not very shocking or startling. It is critical that you understand this dynamic of human communication.

A stereotype that many people have about sales professionals is that we are always trying to put people into a trance to buy things from us. I disagree. I believe our biggest challenge is getting people *out* of a trance! The best way to do that is to offer something startling or bold right up front.

Now you may be saying to yourself, "That's pretty intense! I don't know if I can do that." First of all, understand that your startling statement or question does not need to be quite as dramatic or disturbing as what you see on television or in the movies—certainly not as intense as what you hear about in the news.

You can relate it to your prospect, your market, or your industry, which I will discuss shortly.

But before that, let me ask you a very important question. Is your success an intense topic? Is your ability to live the lifestyle you're committed to—providing the things you want for your family, having the freedom and choices you truly desire—are those things intense? Are being able to communicate more effectively, getting better results, making more money, and having better relationships **all intense topics to you?** I certainly hope your answer to all of those questions is, *"Of course!"* If not, you may be reading the wrong book, and your chances of ever becoming a sales samurai are slim.

Yes, there is a level of intensity here. But would you also agree that there is a lot at stake here as well?

So you want to make either a **bold statement** or ask a **bold question**. Either one can be effective. It is simply a matter of personal choice which one you think is going to be *most* effective. The key is that whichever one you use, you must make sure that it is appropriately startling and dramatic. Let me repeat this. You must go for **startling** and **dramatic**—nothing short of that. So what we're *not* going for is simply interesting, or unique, or professional. Not to say that it cannot or should not be any of those things, but once again, that alone is not enough.

The ultimate goal of the bold question/statement is simply to **get the prospect to want to listen to what you have to say.** That's all we're concerned with at this point. We'll talk about handling her objections and addressing her concerns in another chapter. At this point, you simply want to get her hungry to hear more.

Remember, you don't want to be or sound like everyone else. You want to be different. You want to be what I call the charismatic exception. You want to stand out!

To give you some criteria for how you want it to sound, please read the following list. It is extensive, but you can treat it like a mental buffet. Take what works for you and leave what doesn't.

Your startling statement or question can involve:
- The possibilities of financial gain or financial loss
- Their safety or well being, or the safety and well being of their families
- Personal or professional reputation
- How they'll look in the eyes of other people (personal or professional success)
- The near, medium, or long-term future

- Their time and energy
- Learning from past mistakes
- What you feel their greatest fear(s) might be
- Addressing some key issue in the market place
- What they could lose out on by not taking action—it can involve either possible benefits or possible consequences.
- Something they are looking to gain or experience, or something they are looking to stay away from or avoid

Keep in mind, human beings are motivated primarily by emotion and they justify this with logic. So you would be well served to speak to their emotions.

Doing this well involves what you already know about yourself, the service you provide, your clients or prospects, what they are generally looking for, and the industry or market itself—whether it's the market overall or the current conditions.

So I'm not asking you to think about anything you don't already know, I'm asking you to take a different approach in how you communicate it.

You don't have to memorize all of the above. Simply use it as a guide. The most important thing to keep in mind is that you are not looking to focus simply on facts and details; you are focusing instead on what your prospect is going to gain from listening to you—**their potential benefit**—or what they will lose as a result of *not* listening to you—**their potential loss**.

Let me give you some comparisons of the old, outdated approach versus some **bold statements or questions** that might get your prospects' attention.

Old, outdated approach:

"My company is a consulting and coaching corporation that helps entrepreneurs and sales driven organizations to improve their bottom line results while expanding their perception of what is possible. We work with people in

many different industries and at various levels of experience. Over the years, we have helped many companies like yours step up and get to the next level. We are great at this because we have the experience and know-how. I believe that, given the opportunity, we could have a tremendous impact on your organization. I would truly appreciate the opportunity to discuss this with you in more detail.

How does that sound?"

That sounds fine. But at a certain point, I'm going to put my prospect's feet to sleep with that approach, and they may begin nodding into oblivion. Instead, use a bold statement:

Bold statement:

"I am extremely confident that given the proper support and information, I can help your company improve its bottom line results anywhere from ten to thirty percent within the next six months! And I have some very specific reasons for saying that. Would you like to know why?"

Do you see the difference in these two approaches? Here are some more examples:

1. Old, outdated approach:

"We are a financial services organization that's been around for over fifty years. We have an excellent research department and a strong trading desk. I am a committed, dedicated professional who will go the extra mile for you. I stay on top of the market, and I give my clients quick updates and let them know if anything significant changes within their portfolio. I am confident I would do an excellent job of managing your portfolio. Could I have a few minutes of your time?"

Bold question:

"If you could work with someone who consistently showed you competitive gains in the market [give a specific percentage if you'd like], while protecting your down-side risk and waiting on your account hand over fist as if you were family, would that be worth at least exploring?"

2. Old, outdated approach:

"By staying on top of current trends in the market and listing your property online, we will do a great job of representing your home. We have a twenty-year track record in the industry, and we put a strong emphasis on integrity. We also believe in listening to our clients and servicing their needs at the highest level. If you work with us, you'll be making a very intelligent choice. Our level of service is second to none."

Bold statement:

"If you want to give yourself the best possible chance of selling your home within the next ninety days at a premium price, you need to work with us exclusively! I have some very specific reasons for saying that, which I believe will make all the sense in the world once you've heard them. Can I share those with you briefly?"

3. Old, outdated approach:

"By acquiring a life insurance policy at this time, you will be protecting your family while building up your assets at the same time. The policy I have in mind is suitable for your lifestyle and your current net worth. This way, you know your family will always be covered in case of the worst, God forbid. I will always be here to service your account and I am someone who truly cares about my clients. In working with us, you're working with a winner."

Bold question:

"If I can be blunt, do you realize right now there is a very good chance you are putting your family, the people you care about most, into unnecessary personal and financial danger everyday, simply because you're not taking action on something you should have done years ago? [pause] I know this sounds extreme, but can I explain? This will only take a moment."

4. Old, outdated approach:

"The machines we sell are high quality—top of the line! They are reliable and our brand is a trusted and true name in the industry. In addition, we are a local

vendor, so if anything should ever go wrong, we can get to you quickly. This is a necessary component of your office and you simply cannot do business without it. Let us show you how we can service your office production needs."

Bold statement:

"I am extremely confident I can cut your system downtime anywhere from five to fifteen percent immediately! And I can do this while simultaneously providing you with a superior service plan. Would that be worth hearing about? The reason I say that is ..."

5. Old, outdated approach:

"We have been in the staffing industry for twenty-five years and have worked with ABC corporation, XYZ corporation, and DEF corporation. Our track record speaks for itself. I will work harder for you than anyone else, and I will not stop until I get the job done. You need these positions filled, and we are experts at finding candidates. We have a strong reputation for bringing only the highest quality candidates to the table. I won't let you down."

Bold question:

"If you are not only satisfied but absolutely blown away by the job I do for you over the next ninety days, I won't expect to ever hear from you again! That is how confident I am that I will knock the cover off of the ball here."

You may notice, the old and outdated approach sounds just fine, but that is also one of the potential dangers in using that approach. You run the risk of sounding good enough, or just acceptable, and never really getting through to your prospect. This is a clear example of the difference between good and great—between novice and master—between pupil and samurai.

We're not going for "just fine" here. To a samurai, the word "fine" was an insult. For the samurai, very often the difference between fine and mastery meant the difference between living or dying. More than being just professional, or articulate, or even interesting (which is a step in the right direction), the goal here is for you to communicate in a way that is **dramatic and powerful**—in a way that truly commands people's attention! That alone will give you a *huge* competitive advantage and could make the critical difference.

I am going to ask you to do something here you may not have been expecting. I am going to ask you to use your brain and do some creative thinking. I know; who'd a thought!

I have left some space below for you to write three bold statements and questions. You can write all statements, or all questions, or whatever ratio you want, depending on what feels most beneficial for you and what speaks to your particular style. I encourage you, for now, to write three of each.

If you choose to write directly in the book, I recommend you use pencil in the event you would like to go through it again in the future. I think the best way to do it is to use a separate piece of paper or type on your computer. Ultimately, do whatever works best for you.

If, right now, you are feeling a little lost and thinking to yourself, "There is a lot to take in here," or, "I wish I had someone to answer some of my questions and guide me on this," I have one simple suggestion and one simple question.

The suggestion is to reread and review this material until you begin to feel more comfortable and familiar with it. You may want to pick up my "Samurai of Sales" audio program as well if you don't already have it.

But perhaps most importantly—and with all due respect—**why aren't you working with a professional sales coach?**

Do you have any idea how much time and energy you can save yourself by working with a professional coach? This applies *especially* if you are a veteran of your industry and are looking to step up to the next level or regain a previous level of production. It has been a life-changing experience for many, many people.

For the time being, just do your best and have fun with this. But regardless, *please* do this exercise. This is what allows you to truly integrate this for yourself and use it out there in the world, in live conversations with prospects. Ultimately, you want to have an entire arsenal of bold statements and questions that you can whip out at any stage of the sales dialogue.

Three bold statements:

_____

_____

_____

_____

_____

_____

Three bold questions:

_____

_____

_____

_____

_____

_____

Once you've made a bold statement or asked a bold question, you can follow it up by asking a "leading question" that continues to direct the conversation and shows you are immediately ready to justify what you've just said. I included leading questions in some of the bold questions and statements I listed above. Some examples are:

"Would you like to know why?"

"Would you like me to explain how?"

"Have you heard any of my competitors make that claim?"

"Would you like some proof?"

"Do you know why I say that?"

Or, you can follow up with a leading statement:

"I say that because ..."

"The reason I say that is ..."

For example:

"I say that because we have done it for many other companies in the past."

"I say that because that is exactly what you could be leaving on the table if you continue with your current plan."

"The reason I say that is because current data/statistics/case studies show..."

"I say that because if you just look at our track record..."

CONCLUSION

It's been my experience that the way you say your prospect's name and the startling question or statement you offer within the first 30 seconds of a conversation is at least 80 percent of the game in really grabbing someone's attention and getting her to listen to what you have to say. It can set the tone for the *entire* relationship!

Dissolve the barriers to being heard, and you dissolve the barriers to cultivating lifelong relationships. Doesn't it just make sense to get off to a powerful start? Be someone other people want to listen to and someone other people stand up and take notice of, and distinguish yourself from the competition!

REVIEW:

- When looking to make progress or get better in *any* area, it will often serve you to identify what some of the potential *barriers* are.
- Very often, just being clear on the barrier(s) alone can make all the difference in the world.
- The primary barrier to effective interpersonal communication is that, as an overwhelming rule, people don't listen.
- The best way to become a better listener is to *not* accept everything your prospect is saying at face value.
- Getting someone's attention is critical, because until you have their attention, most if not all of what you say to them is going in one ear and out the other.

- Never underestimate the power of using someone's **name** to get his or her attention.
- In today's market place, and with all of your prospects' internal barriers and defenses up, you must be willing to do nothing less than *startle* your prospect.
- The best way to startle your prospect is with a bold claim or question.
- Once you have gotten your prospect's attention with a bold claim or question, you can then follow up with a leading question and by justifying what you have just said.
- The media is a perfect example of how startling people is an effective way to grab their attention.
- In general, when communicating with people and especially with prospects and clients, you want to be the **charismatic exception.**
- The best way to become great at this skill is to write down various bold questions and statements, and then practice them continuously until they become second nature.

4

QUALIFYING YOUR PROSPECT WITH DIRECTION AND PURPOSE

THE HIDDEN CLOSE

Now we come to one of the most important aspects of persuading *anyone* about any*thing* in life—one of the skills that clearly separates the true Samurai of Sales from the masses—being able to identify what it is that truly drives and motivates the individual you're talking to. What are his values and his priorities? What are the emotions he most wants to experience and the results he most wants to achieve? Likewise, what are the emotions and results he most wants to avoid?

In the world of professional sales, it's also being able to clarify the motivation and authority that any given person has in making an ultimate buying decision—either for themselves, or for their organization. This is known as **qualifying your prospect.**

Why is this important? Because without it, attempting to persuade anyone of anything is sort of like going spear fishing at night. You're shooting blind. You don't know where or what to focus on. Unfortunately, properly qualifying your prospect is something that so many sales professionals overlook when speaking to their prospects.

Let me ask you a simple question. If getting a clear picture of what motivates someone, what makes her tick, and what she wants most will allow you to get drastically better results in much less time and with much less energy, might it be valuable to become versed in that skill, and ultimately to master it? I certainly hope you're saying yes to that.

So let's step to it. The first thing to remember when effectively qualifying your prospect is **questions**—the effective use of questions.

Ask your prospect questions about what she wants as a result of using your product or service, what she wants to avoid, what her primary concern is, what her past experiences have been, and so on. Being a great listener and taking the approach of the **investigative consultant** I referred to in the last chapter is especially critical in this step.

Look at it as if you are looking to understand someone's "persuasion blueprint." You are literally looking to figure out the blueprint in their mind that will allow you to persuade and influence them to make the decisions or take the actions that you want them to.

Yes, I know. This makes sense to you, and the immediate question you ask when you read this is: "Yes, Mitch, but *how*? How do I ask questions or communicate in a way that gives me access to this blueprint?" Well, I'm not a psychic, but I have been training and coaching sales professionals from various industries for over fifteen years, so I do know what questions tend to come up and what to expect.

Understanding that, let's wade right in. First, the fundamentals: below, I have identified the **seven most important questions** to ask in qualifying any prospect:

1. What is most important to you regarding my product/service?

For example:

"What is most important to you regarding the life insurance policy you will choose to protect your family?"

"What is most important to you regarding the real estate agent you are going to work with?"

"What is most important to you regarding the office/duplication/telephone system your company is using?"

Another way you can ask this question is: *"What are you looking to get out of my product/service?"*

2. Who, *in addition to yourself,* needs to be involved in making the final decision?

Be certain to include *"in addition to yourself"* when asking this question, even if you know the person you are speaking to does not have any decision-making power. You never want to demean someone's authority or take him or her out of the equation. Everyone wants to feel important, and you never know what kind of impact they could have by whispering in the ear of their superior, one way or another.

3. Have you spoken with anyone else regarding this?

Be certain to ask this as a closed-ended "yes or no" type question, as opposed to an open-ended (i.e.; "Who else have you spoken with regarding this?") type question. Asking it as an open-ended question assumes he has already spoken with someone else and can suggest that is what he should do.

If your prospect has already spoken with your competition, it's not a problem and is something you can address like anything else. But at the same time, you don't want to encourage it.

Along those lines, if you are concerned that asking this question might drive your prospect to consider speaking with one of your competitors, even though he wasn't planning on it previously, I encourage you to lay that concern to rest.

First off, the *overwhelming majority* of prospects will speak to at least one of your competitors, if not several, whether you bring it up or not. Secondly, if the answer is "no," you can quickly move past it or reassure your prospect about the prudence of dealing with you exclusively. Most importantly, if he *has* spoken with someone else, you *need* to know that—having this information could end up being the critical difference between getting the business or not. For example:

> **You:** "Have you spoken with anyone else regarding this?"
> **Prospect:** "No one."
> **You:** "Great. That makes this a much easier process. How long have you been..."

Or:

> **You:** "Have you spoken with anyone else about this?"
> **Prospect:** "No one. Why, should I be?"
> **You:** "Absolutely not. And I'll tell you why..."

Or:

> **You:** "Well, you could and it's understandable. But what normally ends up happening in that scenario..."
> And paint a picture of unnecessary time and energy being invested, along with resulting confusion and indecision.

Or:

> **You:** "Well, you could. If you did, whom would you consider speaking with?"
> And as they mention potential competitors they would speak with, you say:
> "If you speak with someone from that organization, what they're going to tell you is..."
> And be prepared to professionally downplay that competitor based on what you know to be their perceived style or shortcomings. Of course, if they answer "Yes" to that question,

find out who they've spoken to and be prepared to sell against that provider. Don't start selling against them prematurely, but be prepared to if need be.

4. **How long have you been looking for my product/service?**
For example:
"How long have you been in the market for a new home?"
"How long have you been considering upgrading your system?"
"How long have you been seeking financing?"

5. **How will you know when you've found what you're looking for?**
Be sure not to make the mistake that many sales professionals make when asking this question, which is using the words "exactly" or "precisely." For example, you do *not* want to ask:
"How will you know when you've found exactly what you are looking for?"
The reason is that creates an expectation within your prospect that he will find just that—*precisely* or *exactly* what he wants. And the bottom line is, that is not always the case. As a matter of fact, it is the exception. We live in an imperfect world and what you bring to the table may not have every single specification your prospect desires, but that does not mean that it is not the best possible option for her at that time.

6. **What is the budget that you have allocated for this? What is the highest/lowest you are willing to go?**
If your prospect hesitates in giving you a range or says, "Let's just see what you have to show me first," you can make it easier by offering some examples. Very often, an easy, smooth way to do this is by offering alternatives. For example:
"Were you thinking around___or more like___?"

Keep in mind that when you put these numbers out to your prospect, you are by default suggesting a range. So be strategic with the numbers you offer. You usually want to offer numbers that direct your prospect in the direction you want her to go, whether that is up or down.

As a rule, you want to offer an aggressive number. You want to set the bar high at the beginning. Your prospect can always correct you. Simply suggesting a higher number or range can also plant the seed in the prospect's mind for being open to working bigger.

If, after suggesting a range and offering alternatives, he is still hesitant, you can open him up by explaining it in terms of what is in it for him and why it is in his best interests to be as forthcoming as possible with the information. For example:

"This will allow us to make the best use of your time."

"This will help me to put pencil to paper and get the best possible deal for you."

"With that information, I know how aggressive I can be with__."

You can also ask what she (or her department or company, in the case of corporate prospects) has paid in the past for similar or identical types of products and services.

Once your prospect has given you a number, please understand that this is *not* a time to take what she is saying at face value. Once again, you want to be an **investigative consultant**. I know I have mentioned this term several times, and that is for a reason: because it is so critical! You want to follow up immediately with the question:

"If it hits the nail right on the head/If it's truly exceptional/ if I went above and beyond—is it safe to say we have some wiggle room?" or:

"If it hits the nail right on the head/If it's truly exceptional/ if I went above and beyond—how high could you go?"

Saying this alone can immediately widen the range your prospect gives you in a very subtle and natural way. Notice that it is worded in a way that is gently assumptive and vague. You're actually making a statement, but saying it in a questioning tone of voice. In other words, you're asking an *assumptive question*. These can be very effective. These questions often begin with phrases such as:

"Is it safe to say...?"
"Am I correct in assuming...?"
"Needless to say...?"
"Obviously if we can...?"
"I'm sure you'd agree...?"

If you are speaking with your prospect in person and especially if asking about "wiggle room," this is a good time to give a non-verbal "yes" nod of the head while asking. The power of **non-verbal suggestion**, especially when the prospect already wants to say "yes" on a gut level, can be very effective. If your prospect says, "Yes" to this question, you are already taking control of the conversation and planting the seed.

Do not worry about getting the answer "no" to this question. Very often, you will get something along the lines of, "Yeah, sure. There's always some wiggle room. But it would have to be something truly extraordinary."

If you do get a negative answer, it will rarely be a flat out "no." It will usually sound something like, "Well, it depends," or, "Well, we'll see," or, "I don't know, my budget is kind of tight."

Even if the answer is a "no," you can always revisit. As anyone who has ever been a consumer knows, the fact is that if someone sees something they are truly excited about, there is always some room for wiggle. By asking the question—even if you got a *"no"* answer—you have planted the seed and gotten the prospect prepared for other possible numbers.

The one thing to be aware of if you do get the answer "no" is that you *do not* want to attempt to turn it around or convince the prospect otherwise on the spot. At this point, it is simply a sizing-up and "feeling out" conversation, not an objection. Attempting to get the prospect to change his budget range prematurely may only build the conviction in his mind that he should defend the figure, if for no other reason than just to stay consistent with what he has already said.

Simply leaving it alone would have made it a non-issue.

When qualifying your prospect, asking about budget and buying range with the right emphasis and range up front can pay huge dividends down the line.

7. **"What do you know (or have you heard) about me/my company?"**

Or, if it is a referral:

"What has [the referring party] told you about me/ my company?"

Not only does this give you an opportunity to find out what they know about you, but it *opens the door* in a natural and organic way for you to begin describing yourself, your company, your philosophy, and how you differentiate yourself in the market place after he answers.

GET TO KNOW YOUR PROSPECT

The above seven questions are absolutely critical to understanding your prospect's needs, wants, level of authority, and how to provide him with the best possible solution—no question. And you can of course come up with other variations of these questions, to best suit your particular needs or industry. But if you really want to get inside his mind and endear yourself to him, you must get to know who he is as a person. As corny as this may sound, it is essential, and it consistently distinguishes the most successful performers in any industry from the average.

Find out what he likes and dislikes—what he enjoys doing on weekends, any hobbies he may have, his family, his favorite books, the sports or music he likes, the people he looks up to or who have had a major influence on his thinking, etc. Any time you can gain more insight into what really drives your prospect, in any aspect of his life, you will be more effective at connecting with him and ultimately influencing his decisions. If you think about it, much of what we do **professionally** is for the purpose of being more fulfilled **personally** anyway.

Now, most programs that teach how to qualify your prospect would stop right here. I'm not saying that's bad or wrong, because even what we've covered up to this point is extremely valuable and absolutely *critical*. But I'm about to take it a step further and have you look at an approach for qualifying your clients and your prospects that you wouldn't normally hear about.

How does that sound?

First of all, if you really are doing your job correctly and you're asking a lot of questions (by this, I mean, your predominant tendency is towards questions and anywhere from sixty to as much as eighty percent of what you're saying is in question form), you will *immediately* distinguish yourself from your competition.

Most people are not used to this. They're not used to having someone ask them so many questions.

Above and beyond the standard, fact-finding, "needs analysis" types of questions, your competition isn't asking all that many questions either. Hopefully, that's encouraging to you. Consequently, if you are indeed being the **charismatic exception** I have referred to previously, you want to make sure you prepare your prospect in *advance* for the fact that you will be doing that, and make sure you tell her *why*.

Early on in the process, you want to say something along the lines of:

"I just want to let you know, I ask a lot of questions and maybe more than you're used to. But I do that because I am genuinely interested in hearing what you have to say, and because this conversation is about you, it's not about me."

And there's more. You can also say:

"I really want to find out what is most important to you, and how I can best serve you. So if it's more questions than you're used to, please understand [and this is extremely powerful] *there is a purpose to everything*

I do here and it is so I can best serve you and give you what you're looking for. Is that okay?"

Do not move on until you have her understanding on this. This can be very powerful, because in a very subtle and modest way you're confirming yourself as the expert in that scenario. You are also gaining control of the conversation. You may want to read the above sentences to yourself a few times. This is what I call a **pre-frame**—where you **plant a seed** in the mind of your prospect in advance about how she is going to perceive or feel about something you will be doing later on.

You may have noticed that I have used the expression "plant a seed" several times in this chapter already. That is because you can create a very strong predisposition in the mind of your prospect while **simultaneously qualifying** her and finding out what her primary motivation is—all at the same time!

In other words, **you can uncover her persuasion blueprint while directing how she will feel about your offering in advance — simultaneously!** Is that pretty useful? Let's take a look at that:

The questions that direct your prospect's focus and plant the seed are usually hypothetical "either/or" type questions—although they don't have to be. You want to give him an either/or choice and you obviously want to direct the question in a way that keeps it a legitimate question while directing him towards giving the answer you want. Some questions you can ask are:

"When making a decision like this one, are you generally more concerned with getting the cheapest price up-front, or the long-term performance down the line?"

Notice, I did not say the "best" price. I said the "cheapest" price.

How do you think most people will answer this question? The long-term value, of course. But as simple as it may seem, asking this kind of guided question can pay big dividends down the line if your prospect is looking to procrastinate on making a buying decision on account of cost.

It's kind of like a boxer who goes to the body on his opponent early on in a fight. It usually pays benefits in the later rounds.

And if someone is *not* going to answer that way—if someone would just flat out say, "No I'm more interested in getting the cheapest price possible, above all other concerns,"—while that may be the exception, wouldn't you want to know that answer in advance?

And if they try to stay neutral on their answer, your job is to put it into "either/or" terms. So you can say:

"I understand. But if you had to choose."

"If you had to choose between something that was clearly superior but that you'd have to wait longer for, or getting something more quickly but which may not be as dependable, which would you prefer?"

"Are you of the belief that cheaper is always the best way to go?"

"Are you expecting to get *every* feature you have outlined here within the budget you have specified?"

"Are you looking to be conservative, aggressive, or some combination of both?"

"When you see what you want, do you tend to procrastinate, or are you usually pretty good at pulling the trigger?"

"Are you a moment-to-moment kind of guy/girl, or do you tend to look at the bigger picture?"

"If someone is showing you performance and getting you the results you want, do you tend to bust their chops over nickels and dimes?"

As you have probably noticed, questions like these begin to generate graduated levels of consensus and commitment well before an actual buying decision is called for. In answering these questions one way or another, the prospect is making a statement about themselves and how they operate. As I am writing these sentences, I wish I could find the best way to articulate how truly powerful and influential questions like these can be when asked naturally and early on in the dialogue with your prospect.

If your prospect has trouble or is hesitant in answering "either/or" type questions, you explain why you are asking the question and then you simply repeat the question. Very often when you go that little extra step in a conversation, that's when you turn someone around or get him to give you that answer you're looking for.

A great way to have your prospect answer questions like these is to say:

"I don't want to come to any flash judgments about you, or how you operate because sometimes what we think is obvious is not—it's just downright wrong. I'd rather be sure than to assume."

If you think about it, this is a great perspective to come from when dealing with people in general.

"You strike me as..."

There are seeds you can plant in the form of statements in a nonchalant "by the way" sort of manner during appropriate times in the conversation. These will create what I call **self-concept consistency.** Remember, people will usually want to remain consistent with the things they say to be true about themselves — and will act accordingly. Planting the seeds will usually begin with the statement, "You strike me as someone who..." For example:

"You strike me as someone who...
...means what he says."
...doesn't like to waste time."
...doesn't sweat the small stuff for the bigger picture."

...doesn't save pennies only to waste dollars."

...understands that achieving total perfection in any endeavor is extremely rare."

You always want to follow one of these questions up with:

"Is that true?"

"Am I right on that?"

"Is that accurate?"

"Would you agree?"

And then **let the prospect talk about himself!** If he agrees, that's great. If he disagrees or gives a different answer, that's even better. You are learning about your prospect and how he views himself, and he is creating self-concept consistency for himself, one way or the other. So, for example:

"[Prospect's first name], you strike me as a man of your word. Am I right about that?"

How will someone usually answer that question? "Well, yeah, of course!" Once someone answers, "yes," to that question, do you think he will be more motivated and feel more internal pressure to adhere to any agreements or commitments he makes to you? You better believe it!

How often will someone answer "no" to that question? Probably not that often. But if someone does answer "no," don't you think it would be a good thing to know up front? Some other examples are:

"You strike me as someone who...

...Is sharp enough to take good advice when it's given. Am I on target with that?"

...Doesn't believe in wasting time. Am I right?"

...Believes in learning from her mistakes. Yes?"

...Will be flexible if it's going to get you what you want. Correct?"

...Heeds good advice when it's given. Yes?"

There are a slew of examples you could use here, depending on your particular industry and set of outcomes.

Lead him—bit by bit, step by step—to commit to certain expectations of what he will or will not do, and who he, as an individual, is or is not.

If you are thinking to yourself that some of the questions or statements I have mentioned are a bit obvious or direct, do not be deterred. Because remember, it is your job to begin to frame and direct the conversation with your prospect from the very beginning.

If you are being real with this person and have rapport and communicate naturally, *it is no big deal.* This is business, not family talk at the barbecue (although the two do not need to be mutually exclusive). Most importantly, perhaps, is to keep in mind that this is not as difficult as you might think, because remember what everyone's favorite topic is? *Themselves!*

Any chance you give her to talk about her favorite topic will normally be very well received. Remember that people want to remain consistent with the things they say, especially when they are about themselves. I am officially challenging you to try this in conversation with your prospects, especially when qualifying them or conducting fact finders, and watch what happens. This approach has had a profound impact on many of the coaching and consulting clients I've worked with over the years.

Keep in mind, your mission is to do this subtly, throughout the course of normal conversation, during intervals or transitions where it is normal or natural. You can also capitalize on opportunities in the conversation by inserting these questions when the appropriate topics come up. With this approach, you have to exercise a certain level of common sense and sound judgment. Make sure you have rapport first!

This topic reminds me of a routine I once heard from the actor Steve Martin back when he was doing standup comedy. He spoke about how he used to struggle with getting the order right with women he was trying to pick up. He'd walk up to a woman he'd never met before and say: "Hi! Was it good for you too?" Or they would wake up the morning after, and then he would try to get her drunk.

The timing must be right and the rapport must be there.

Please understand that this process is not as overt or obvious as asking standard "fact-finding" type questions. If you're not careful with your implementation of these techniques, it can come across the wrong way and possibly be perceived as manipulation. But using these techniques and approaches effectively and in the natural rhythm of conversation can be *precisely* what separates you from your competition and be what gives you your competitive edge. This is a clear example of what separates the samurai from the novice practitioner.

This is how you begin to get others to do what you want them to do, seemingly effortlessly at times. They won't even know why they are doing it; they simply feel compelled to act in a certain way, apparently for their own internal reasons. Yet those reasons were implanted and magnified by the use of some strategically positioned questions or statements by you earlier in the conversation. I implore you—use this!

You can also ask your prospect to share experiences in which he worked hard towards something or relied on someone, but then at some point was let down by a situation or by another person who did not maintain their end of the bargain. This helps to reinforce any commitments or promises *he* made to *you* earlier on in the sales process. Your prospect (as a rule) is not going to want to be the person who does not keep commitments or who isn't loyal.

Another great approach is to remind your prospect of times when he tried to do something on his own but would have been better off handing it over to an expert, and paid the price for it. Some examples: auto repair, home improvement, taxes, financial decisions, investment decisions, physical fitness or working out, driving directions, or technology. Most, if not all of us, have made one or several mistakes in at least one of these areas as a result of trying to be an expert when we are not. You can read *Turning Objections into Transactions* to learn more about this.

These questions can help guard you against potential objections down the line, for example those that would revolve around paying too much in commission or those that arise from the prospect wanting to do it themselves, etc. A few strategically placed questions like these can dilute those objections or even prevent them from ever coming up in the first place.

A great technique for getting people to be more open to answering those questions or to share experiences is to first share experiences *you've* had or mistakes you have made in the past. As long as they are genuine and legitimate, you can prepare some stories in advance. A great side benefit to this is that it allows you to be humble and vulnerable to a degree, and it allows your prospect to feel like he is getting to know you better. This can be what brings down your prospect's defenses and truly has him open up.

So for example, if you are going to ask someone about a time they tried to do something on their own but it backfired because they should have asked an expert, you can tell them about a time when that happened to you or describe a bad decision you previously made. Once again, you want to be subtle with this and use your common sense.

For me, a great example I like to give is when I hired a large, household name, factory-type of tax service, which shall remain nameless. They charged a cheap fee, comparatively, to handle my taxes, when at that time I would have been *much* better off working with a CPA who specialized in working with entrepreneurs and small business owners like myself—one who really understood my situation and all of the benefits I could take advantage of as well as what to be aware of. And let me just say, I paid a *huge* price as a result of not doing that. Of course, when speaking with my prospect, I would get into detail and clarify just how much it cost me.

After telling a story like that, I would follow up with a question such as:

"Have you ever had that type of experience yourself?"
"Have you ever made a mistake like that?"
"Have you ever done something like that?"
"Have you ever been through anything like that yourself?"

You will be amazed! Some people just can't wait to join in on that conversation and start talking about themselves. Others can't wait to start complaining. If you do this effectively and subtly, they'll have no idea what you're doing. And that's not a bad thing! Subtlety is an art, not a sin.

This brings me to a very important point and a *critical* distinction to make when using these tools: if you have your prospects' best interests in mind and you are coming from a place of integrity and service and doing the right thing, there is nothing wrong with having an agenda in the conversation! Gandhi had an agenda. Martin Luther King had an agenda. Mother Theresa had an agenda.

It is actually very simple. Not necessarily easy, but indeed simple. Get to know your prospects, what drives their behavior, how they view themselves, and what they are looking for—and you will be a master at persuading them to take the actions you want them to. It will be yet another critical step taken on the path to becoming a true Samurai of Sales. If you don't do this, you will forever struggle with getting inside their mind and getting them to do what you want them to.

I challenge you—I dare you—to become great at this!

REVIEW:

- Being able to identify what drives and motivates someone is critical in being able to persuade him/her of anything.
- In the world of professional sales, you must also identify the level of authority and the decision-making ability your prospect possesses as quickly as possible.
- The single most important tool in effectively qualifying your prospect is asking effective *questions*.
- The person who is asking the questions in a conversation is the one who is in control of that conversation.
- Your goal is to figure out their *persuasion blueprint* while simultaneously *planting seeds* in their mind about how they will view your product or service.

- Eighty percent of the "close" actually occurs while qualifying your prospect, developing rapport, building consensus, and creating commitment.
- Getting progressively deeper levels of commitment and "self-concept consistency" gives you progressively more leverage in the conversation.
- The key is to do this subtly, as a natural part of the conversation—not as a "technique."
- A great way to plant seeds through the use of questions is to have the prospect share his/her own experiences.

5

SLICING THROUGH
OBJECTIONS: PART I

A REVOLUTIONARY APPROACH TO
HANDLING SALES RESISTANCE

I'd like to discuss what many sales professionals consider to be *the* most important aspect of sales and very often the most challenging as well. This can apply to any industry and any stage of the sales cycle.

Question: *What is usually the greatest barrier that stands between what you propose and what your prospect actually does?*

Objections!

The specter that strikes fear into the hearts—and pain into the heads—of so many sales professionals.

The prospect's objections arise from his concerns with what you are suggesting or what you want him to do. This topic seems to be a thorn in the side of so many sales professionals. They say things like:

"Boy, this job would be great if it weren't for all the objections."
"Boy, this job would be great if it weren't for all the sales resistance."

"Boy, this job would be great if it weren't for all these people saying 'no' to me."

Being totally candid here, have you ever said that to yourself at one time or another? Most of us have.

I'm here to tell you that if you are saying this to yourself on a consistent basis, **you have picked a very strange career to get into!** News flash: dealing with objections is your job! That's like a surgeon saying: *"Boy, this doctor stuff would be great if it weren't for all the surgeries I have to perform."*

Others, especially those who are new to their respective industries, are just downright afraid of objections. They associate objections with emotions like fear, intimidation, discouragement, anxiety, doubt, and in some cases even a sense of loathing. This can be a *huge* barrier. So let's take a look at this.

First of all, what are objections?

One common definition is that objections are simply questions in disguise—a request for more information—and I believe this is valid. But in my experience, when you boil it down to the simplest common denominator, objections are really nothing more than a **difference in opinion.** The objection itself is one party expressing to another that they don't agree and *why*.

From a standpoint of identifying the barrier (which is a common theme in my teaching approach), would you like to know why most people, to one degree or another, struggle with this critical skill—what holds most people back from greatness in this area? Are you ready for a tremendously deep and profound answer?

It's because they don't **enjoy** it.

That's it! You might have been hoping for a huge epiphany or some ultra-scientific breakthrough, but the bottom line is that the degree to which you struggle with objections is the degree to which you do not *enjoy* the process of *handling* objections.

You may be saying to yourself, "Well, that's sort of simple. There must be more to it." As I often like to say: simple, yes, but not necessarily easy. In theory, lifting a five-thousand-pound boulder is simple.

We have been socialized and conditioned to believe that differences in opinion are a bad thing. We think it's bad when someone disagrees with us, tells us that we're wrong, or tries to shoot down our ideas. We think we have done something wrong when someone says "no" to what we are suggesting or proposing.

Our parents trained us in this way when we were children, as a way to control us. They did so for one main reason: *they had to!* As cute and adorable as little children are, could you imagine the havoc they would bring upon themselves and on others if left to their own devices? It's a bit scary to contemplate.

As a result, our parents or guardians could not simply be satisfied with a difference in opinion. They had to have some real pain, some real fear, loaded into the process of challenging their opinion. And this continued with other authority figures in our lives: teachers, coaches, bosses, instructors, religious figures, etc. Throughout your entire life, almost everyone who has tried to control you—whether with good intentions or not—has done their absolute best to make you want to avoid confronting them or challenging their opinions.

Through no fault of your own, you already start off *way* behind the eight ball in this area. I'm not talking about some traumatic childhood experience that has scarred you for life (and I'm not downplaying the significance of such an experience either) but rather I'm talking about a systematic conditioning over an extended period of time. Did you know that according to a study conducted at UCLA, the "typical" one-year-old child hears the word *"no!"* over four hundred times in a single day?

As a result, most of us don't enjoy having to deal with differences in opinion—people disagreeing with us, telling us we are wrong, or shooting down our ideas—also known as **rejection.** But would you agree that what may have served to control or protect us as children, may not necessarily be what serves or empowers us as adults? As a professional, fear of rejection will hinder you in moving forward powerfully to grow your business, because you must be able to handle the inevitable rejection you are going to face along the way. As a *sales* professional, fear of rejection can be lethal. And it often is.

The bottom line is at some point in your sales career, dealing with massive rejection will be required if you are to reach the heights of "star" status and become a true sales master. Below, I have listed an acronym I call **"MR. COR"** that I believe summarizes this point rather well:

MR. COR: Massive Rejection Creates Outstanding Results

Massive

Rejection

Creates

Outstanding

Results

It is a fact of life and one of the pure fundamentals of success. In business, this rejection usually takes the form of objections or sales resistance. I'd like you to think about this next question:

How often do you struggle with practicing or learning how to do something you absolutely *love*, something you think is the most amazing thing on the planet?

I'm not saying you get it right the first time or that you don't hit barriers along the way or anything to that effect. I'm simply asking how often do you really struggle with taking something on and *attacking* it when you truly love it? You go full steam ahead and do it with a passion, don't you? When you think about the topics you are absolutely passionate about—the things that really get you jazzed when you wake up in the morning and that you can't wait to get started on, that *inspire* you—how often does the thought of handling an unlimited number of objections and consistent rejection register on that list?

If you truly love something, if you consider it a privilege to be able to do it, if you think it's the most amazing thing since sliced sushi (I rarely eat bread), do you usually have a whole lot of trouble practicing it or finding out what you have to do to be around it more often? Are there other things in your life that require a similar (or greater) level of skill or aptitude for handling objection, which you've really taken on, practiced aggressively and perhaps even mastered?

If you're at least fairly proficient at handling objections, you already know that being effective with this skill is actually pretty simple. Once again, not always *easy*, but certainly simple. All we're talking about is ***knowing and understanding how to respond when someone says "no" with a reason attached to it!*** When you look at it objectively (no pun intended), this is all it is!

So I have a question:

Why don't more sales professionals, whose careers, livelihood and personal incomes depend so heavily on being able to handle objections, practice and truly become samurai in this area?

It's because they don't *enjoy* it! They don't have a love for it! If you think all you need to be great at this skill are the words and closes, I am here to politely tell you that you are wrong. If you're struggling to accept this— good. Just bear with it for a little while and let it settle in. Seriously think about it.

I'd like you to think of some skills you've learned and mastered that are clearly just as difficult—if not more so—than learning how to respond to an objection. Some examples are:

Skiing
Ice-skating
Virtually any sport Martial Arts
A musical instrument
A foreign language
Various computer functions

What's more difficult: learning how to respond when someone says "no," or learning how to speak German fluently when you've never spoken it before? Think about that quantitatively for a moment.

There is also performing, acting, and how about people who learn how to program or network computers? How about graphic designers, interior designers, gardeners, surgeons, attorneys, artists, architects, yoga instructors, and all the other skilled specialists? Do you really think those things are so much easier than learning a simple system of how to communicate and what to say in response to the word *"no?"*

It's simple—you don't enjoy having to deal with it. You associate it with things like dread, inconvenience, looking bad, or low self-esteem. If your ego is being challenged right now, or if perhaps you're reminded of some ways in which you have not been showing up as powerfully as you know you could in this area, please believe me when I tell you this is a good thing; it means you're on the verge of a breakthrough.

The key to mastering objections is learning to absolutely *love* handling objections. After reading that, you might have just pulled what I call a "Scooby-Doo." Do you remember Scooby's trademark expression: *"Harrugh?"* in the tone of *"What?"* If you responded that way, that's why you're struggling with objections.

I'd like to ask you a question, and you may want to take a moment before answering this:

Do you honestly, sincerely, on a gut level, *love* handling objections?

I want to be clear. I'm not asking whether you don't mind handling them, accept them as a necessary evil, or think some are easier than others. I'm not asking whether you occasionally enjoy them; for example, *"There are much more difficult things I could be dealing with... beats digging ditches..."* I'm not even asking whether you think you're good at handling them.

What I'm asking is, when someone hands you an objection—when they have just disagreed with you, said "no," shot you down, and been very clear that they have no interest in listening to you ever again—on a deep sincere, gut level, in the core of your being, do you get genuinely excited, happy and literally thankful about just having heard that objection?

If you have just answered that question with a clear, enthusiastic, unabashed, "Yes!" or "Absolutely!—which, to be candid, is quite rare—then all you need to do is continue to improve your skills and stay sharp and you're home free, which shouldn't be much of a challenge because you already enjoy this process.

But if you answered "no," which is the case for most people, the degree of your aversion to dealing with objections is directly correlated to the degree with which you struggle to *handle* them—and, ultimately, it hinders your chances of ever becoming a samurai in this critical area. Why should objection-handling be any different from anything else in life?!!! If you want to be truly great at it, you need to have a love for it. And please keep in mind, the main premise of this book, as evident in its title, is not to simply get better or marginally improve your skills; but to reach *true mastery*.

Right now you may be saying, *"Well, that's not possible, Mitch—to love handling objections. It's not natural. It goes against human nature,"* or something to that effect. If that is the case, I have one response:

Oh yes it is possible!

Take myself as an example. I have a confession to make. *I love handling objections!* Please just stay with that for a moment—let it sink in. Very often, when I say that to sales professionals, it's as if I just confessed to an addiction.

At the very least, people look at me as if I have three heads. The question I asked above about what gets you jazzed when you wake up in the morning? I really do get jazzed about handling objections.

I tell you that I went from a place of being *literally terrified* of dealing with sales resistance and rejection to absolutely loving it—in less than two years. In the introduction of this book, I spoke a bit about my journey to sales mastery. If you'll indulge me, I'd like to go into a bit more detail to illustrate the point I am making here.

When I first got into professional sales, after a brief stint (about one year) in the office-solutions industry, I was cold-calling as a stockbroker, pitching stocks to individual investors and making well over six hundred dials a day. I was dealing with massive, rapid-fire rejection.

I can remember it vividly. My voice would tighten up, I'd start each call like a baritone and by the time the call was finished I would sound like a soprano— and not the ones from television. I would get thirsty after three or four presentations. My breathing would get shallow. I would expect to be unsuccessful before I even got on the phone.

It was demoralizing and discouraging. But I *knew* I could be great at it, because I saw people who were no more intelligent or talented than I was doing extremely well. By engaging in a process of never-ending growth, development and learning (which continues to this day), I completely transformed myself. I became a sales shogun, which loosely translated is a master samurai amongst other samurai. I'm not saying it happened overnight or that there was any magic bullet, but I did *whatever I had to*, to make the transition.

In my candid opinion and without ego, I am one of the best in the world at successfully dealing with objections and laying them to rest. It's been said that my telephone is the place where objections come to die. And I absolutely *love* the process!

Just think about that type of transformation!

So it is possible. And I promise you I am only one example; I know many other people who have been through a similar process. If hearing the word *"love"* in regards to dealing with objections intimidates you or seems too much or somehow rubs you the wrong way, then good! It's good to have your current way of thinking challenged every now and then.

If, right now, the concept of actually *loving* objections is too extreme, let's work on just learning to *enjoy* or even *embrace* objections. Perhaps now is the time to have your comfort zone stretched just a bit. Fair enough?

With this is mind, I have a question: **what's possible for you in your own life in regards to this incredibly important topic?**

Let's take an even closer look at this. **I'd like you to envision the situation(s) or scenario(s) you are usually in when dealing with objections.** It could be in the office, out in the field, in the show room, on the phone, whichever. You may want to take a break from this reading, close your eyes for a moment, and really concentrate. Be as clear and as vivid as possible when envisioning this.

I want you to think about your internal dialogue here for a moment. That inner voice you have that is constantly conversing with you. You know the one I'm talking about. If you just asked yourself, "What inner voice?"—That's the voice. If you'll notice, it's constantly with you.

Being totally honest and candid with yourself, what are some negative things you tend to say to yourself when someone hands you an objection? I'm talking about your instinctive response in that first split second, when you first hear the objection, not what you try to tell yourself through positive self-talk after the fact. Be brutally honest with yourself.

And once again, I want to caution any sales veterans who are reading this right now. This applies double to you because you have probably deluded yourself into believing you have this completely handled. Let me reiterate: **you never have this completely handled!** You must always keep your mental blade sharp. By nature, it is a never-ending process.

For veterans, sales resistance may be even more challenging, because as a rule it is not coming from cold calls or nameless, faceless prospects, but rather from people with whom you have an existing relationship or a history, making it even more difficult.

I encourage you to do some word association with the following statements. In other words, when you read these objections, imagine you are hearing them in real-life selling situations. Notice the *very first response* that pops into your mind, and then write it down. Pay attention to impulse, not to what you think you "should" be thinking. And once again, be brutally honest: write down the impulse answer you get immediately after reading the objection:

"I'm not interested!"
"Not now."
"This isn't a good time."
"Can you get back to me in a couple of weeks?"

(Quick side note: Isn't it amazing how many people seem to be in meetings or on a conference call when you contact them to present your product or service? I haven't quite figured out that natural phenomenon yet.)

"Your price/commission/premium is way too high!"

"Your competition's price/commission/premium is lower."

"I'm going to handle this myself."

"We've decided to handle this internally."

"I just don't like the market right now. Get back to me in a few months."

"I need to speak to some of your competitors first."

"It's just not in our budget."

"You're just another sales person who wants my money!"

"First I need to speak with my ...

>   *...partner*
>   *...team*
>   *...wife*
>   *...husband*
>   *...attorney*
>   *...accountant*
>   *...financial advisor*
>   *...astrologer*
>   *...cat*
>   *...goldfish*
>   *...neighborhood wino..."*

(Yes, I'm having fun with that one, but sometimes it is absolutely ridiculous whom some prospects claim they need to speak to before being able to make a buying decision.)

"Please just send me some information, and if I'm interested I'll get back to you."

"I need to do some more research on this first."

"I need to bounce this off of corporate."

"I need to wait for our next budget meeting."

"I need to talk to purchasing."

Some of these objections apply to B2C (business to consumer), and some apply to B2B (business to business). But they can be barriers regardless.

Some examples of limiting responses to these objections that have come up for me personally in the past are:

"Ooh, not again!"
"Why is she being so difficult?!!!"
"Why is he such a jerk?!!!"
"Doesn't this ever get any easier?!!!"
"Why does this have to be so difficult?!!!"
"That's not good."
"I was afraid he was going to say that."
"Can ONE person just say 'yes'?!!!"
"What's your problem?!!!"
"!@#$%^&+!" (You can figure that one out)*
"Jeez!"
"Damn! What do I say here?"

And there's more.

This may not all be politically correct, but I want you to be able to learn about how it really is from my past experience; and anyway, we know the mind doesn't always think in politically correct terms (which could be the understatement of the year!) You can use my answers if they are genuine for you.

Please take a few minutes to write down your responses. And please really do it. Make this reading worth your while!

I have had experiences reading a book such as this when I have taken a break in the action to answer questions or do an exercise and what started as a simple answer or quick thought turned into an intense, thought-provoking personal session with myself, where I wrote down many answers or many approaches and gained some real clarity. I was able to make some tremendous distinctions, simply as a result of delving into a particular topic. If, in putting a few minutes aside to answer, it should turn into more, and you realize at one point there is so much more to write or think about, then just go for it!

So what came up for you? Did any negative responses come to mind? Did any positive responses come to mind? Obviously, what we want to address here are the *negative* responses, because those are what can hold you back. And there are usually a lot more of those. So I have some important questions for you:

While these responses are understandable, do they give you what you want? Do they support you in really stepping up and attacking objections with enthusiasm when they cross your path? Do they support you in really jumping into the process of mastering this skill and of keeping your mind fine-tuned in this area? I think we can agree that the answer to *all* of those questions is, "Absolutely not."

I want you to ponder the question below:

What would life be like if you associated handling objections to a deep sense of *pleasure?*

Yes, you read that correctly. What if—instead of what you just wrote down when you heard an objection—your first gut reaction was along the lines of, "*Yes!*" or, "*Awesome!*" or, "*Thank you!*"

Would that be empowering?

Are you open to considering a completely new perspective for yourself in this area?

I would like you to think about some *new* impulse responses you can create in your mind.

What are some new responses you can say to yourself in that moment, in that split second, that are real and that ring true when you hear objections? Keep this simple. It can be just one word; for example, *Excellent! Great! Perfect!* Or just one short statement or question, like: "*That is absolutely right,*" or, "*I am glad you said that,*" or, "*Thank you!*"

Would you like to know what one of *my* favorites is?

"*Awesome!*"

Simple, but incredibly powerful.

For example, I do a lot of work as a corporate consultant and executive coach, and early on in my career when I was making a name for myself, I'd often be confronted with objections like: *"Mitch, I think you're great and I'm sure you can have a positive impact, but I'm just not interested in doing business with you right now..." "We do all of our training in-house..." "We don't have anything allocated in our budget right now for training or consulting..."* and so on.

While most people would say, *"Oh boy, here we go again..."* or, *"What do I say now?"* or, *"Why is this guy being so difficult?"* etc., in my mind, I was literally saying:

"Awesome! This is great! I've just been given an objection! I now have a challenge to rise to! I am so in my element! This is what I put my suit and tie on for in the first place! I now have something to do with myself!"

I realize this may seem a bit over the top when first reading it, but I want you to really step into this and be open to it. If practicing this could create a life-changing transformation for you, would it be worth it? How else will you ever create life-changing breakthroughs and paradigm shifts if you're not willing to step outside of your comfort zone and try something new?

I'm now going to feed you the same objections again, as listed above. I want you to put yourself in that moment, that place or situation you are usually in (or one of the several you tend to be in) when you are dealing with the brunt of your sales resistance and confronted with these obstacles. When you read the objection, please respond in your mind with a positive, empowering response.

Again, don't make this fluff. Use something you could really see yourself responding with in that moment.

To be absolutely clear, let me give you a list of some possible responses:

Awesome!
Excellent!
Thank you!
That's great!
I hear you!

Fantastic!
I was hoping you'd say that!
Perfect!
I got it!
Nice!

There are more, and I encourage you to come up with some of your own. I clearly don't have a monopoly on the empowered responses you can use. And if you are smiling to yourself because of how out of the box it is, then great! Maybe it's time for a new perspective.

Even if it's a bit of a stretch right now, please really do it and do it with intensity. Please come back with an empowered impulse response to each of the objections below:

"I'm not interested!"

_____

_____

Empowered response!

"Your price/commission/fee/premium is way too high!"

_____

_____

Empowered response!

"Your competitor's price/commission/fee/premium is lower!"

_____

_____

Empowered response!

"Please call me back in a couple of weeks. Not right now."

_____

_____

Empowered response!

"I just don't like the market right now. Get back to me in a few months."

_____

_____

Empowered response!

"I need to speak to some of your competitors first."

_____

_____

Empowered response!

"It's just not in our budget."

_____

_____

Empowered response!

"I don't have time for this right now!"

_____

_____

Empowered response!

"You're just another sales person who wants my money!"

_____

_____

Empowered response!

"I need to speak with my [wife, husband, attorney, accountant, astrologer, cat, etc.] first."

_____

_____

Empowered response!

"Please just send me some information, and if I'm interested I'll get back to you."

Empowered response!

"I need to bounce this off of corporate."

Empowered response!

"I need to wait until our next budget meeting."

Empowered response!

"I need to speak with purchasing first."

Empowered response!

Are you noticing any shifts? Are you making any distinctions? I encourage you to repeat this process several times, and I want to point out that if you truly want this exercise to have an impact and make a difference, you must embrace it and be willing to practice it.

If you think this is interesting, you should see what we do at my live events! I literally walk my students through interactive exercises where they recondition their minds, bodies and emotional beings on a cellular level to transform how they react to objections and sales resistance. It creates a huge paradigm shift!

Here's the key. *Practice it.* For starters, you can re-read this section, and every time you hear an objection, just repeat to yourself the new, supportive, empowering response. You can say it to yourself, or you can say it out loud. You can also role-play this with someone else.

I'd like you to consider this. What would your life be like if, as a sales professional or entrepreneur, you were walking around, waiting, *eager and excited* about the possibility of people handing you objections or sales resistance? Think about how powerful that would be!

What an empowered, aware and alert state of mind you would exist in. If you are not already in that place, I challenge you to create it for yourself.

Because when you are, your life overall becomes much more enjoyable and at times even effortless. And perhaps most valuable of all, you have paved a clear path to the destination we call Samurai of Sales.

REVIEW:

- Most sales professionals consider dealing with objections and sales resistance to be the most challenging aspect of professional sales.
- The irony is that this is also the most important component of being successful in professional sales.
- An "objection" is nothing more than a difference in opinion being expressed.
- The main reason most sales professionals struggle with handling objections effectively is because they *do not enjoy it.*
- We have been conditioned from a very early age to believe that dealing with rejection and hearing the word *"no"* is a bad and unpleasant thing.
- The key to mastering objection-handling is to associate a deep sense of pleasure with it and even harbor a love for it.
- The first step in learning to enjoy objections is to identify exactly what you tend to say to yourself internally, in that split second when you're first presented with an objection.

- The key is to replace negative, unsupportive, disempowering responses with supportive, proactive responses that will propel you forward powerfully.
- You are at your best when you respond proactively—not just internally to yourself, but out loud to your prospect as well.
- Have fun with objections!

6

SLICING THROUGH OBJECTIONS: PART II

WHAT TO SAY AND HOW TO SAY IT

Any study in mastering objections is incomplete without some specific guidelines on what to say and how to say it. What's mentioned in this chapter is what I have found to be the most powerful and effective things you can say to (or ask) your prospect to create a shift and lay their objections to rest. Some of it is very basic, and some of it is a completely new and innovative way of approaching objection handling—the basic principles of which were laid out in the previous chapter. The bottom line is that everything described below is incredibly effective and gets results.

YOU MUST EMPATHIZE WITH YOUR PROSPECT

"When someone is giving you his opinion, you should receive it with great gratitude even though it is worthless. If you don't, he will not tell you the things that he has seen and heard about."
- HAGAKURE, *THE BOOK OF THE SAMURAI*

This critical element of mastering objection-handling is something you may have heard before, but it is absolutely *essential* if you are going to be great at this, and I would be remiss if I chose to ignore it. It is that you must *empathize* with your prospect.

The key to this is when someone hands you an objection, you don't want to butt heads with him. You don't want to make him wrong or make him feel as if he's not being heard. No one likes to be dismissed or negated. You want to *align* with him and be on his side.

Doesn't that just make sense? You'd be amazed at how overlooked this one simple tool is—even by experienced salespeople!

You empathize by saying one of the following four phrases:

I appreciate ...
I respect ...
I understand ...
I agree ...

If you are new in your respective industry, and you have not been practicing this, you *must* begin to put this in your repertoire. If not, you will be making your life as a sales professional *much* more difficult than it needs to be.

If, on the other hand, you are already experienced, it doesn't matter how many times you may have heard this before or how rudimentary it may be, because remember the fundamental I shared about fundamentals? ***There are no new fundamentals! And fundamentals must be practiced consistently!***

Remember that very often there is a big difference between common sense and common practice. As the old saying goes, *"What you don't use, you lose."*

Do you *always* execute this perfectly every time out? I'd say for most people, the chances of that being the case are rare. And regardless of how well you do or don't execute this now, would you agree that reinforcing it and making it stronger will only *improve* your skills and strengthen your response patterns?

The words *respect, agree, understand* and *appreciate* should become common words in your vocabulary.

THE TWO WORDS YOU MUST AVOID

Next, if I could share with you a tool that would help you address and turn around any point of view, difference in opinion, or belief in a way that was incredibly effective and powerful and yet was also very respectful, low-key and subtle all at the same time—would that be incredibly useful?

I certainly hope you answered *"yes"* to that one.

It's simply a matter of developing a deep awareness and sensitivity to the use of two words in particular, and then replacing them. These two words can very often *singlehandedly* blow sales out of the water and cause you to miss tremendous opportunities.

The words are **"but"** and **"however."**

How does this sound:

"I really like you, *but...*" Or:

"I really like you, *however...*"

Anything you say after the words *"but"* or *"however"* is going to sound like a negation of what you just said. Correct? You could have said the nicest thing to someone, *but* if you immediately follow it up with the words "but" or "however," anything you say afterwards is going to contradict it. **Even if what you're saying is a compliment!**

These two words kill sales and they destroy rapport! They negate any agreement or empathy you may have just offered. And it is amazing how often people use these words when communicating with prospects and clients.

You can replace the words "but" or, "however" with **"and."** I'd like you to compare the following pairs of statements: "I like you, *but* you're really intense,"

Versus,

"I like you, *and* you're really intense." Or:

"I like you; however, you're really intense," Versus,

"I like you, and you're really intense."

The first of each pair sound like a put down or negation, while the second one actually sounds like a compliment. All because of changing *one* word! Think about that! Be very aware of those words and how often you use them.

Similarly, think about how that applies when looking to empathize with a prospect:

"I understand exactly how you feel, ***but*** ..." Or:

"I can appreciate what you're saying, ***however*** ..." Versus:

"I understand exactly how you feel, ***and*** ..."

"I can appreciate what you're saying, ***and***..."

This is a little thing that can make a *big* difference. As Harvey Mckay likes to say: *"The little things are not a lot. The little things are everything."*

So when you use the words of empathy I described above, you always want to follow them up immediately with the word *"and."*

"I appreciate ***and*** ..."

"I respect ***and*** ..."

"I understand ***and*** ..."

"I agree ***and*** ..."

Now, I want to make one important distinction here. It is okay to use the words *"but"* and *"however"* when negating *yourself.* For example, "I was thinking about going to the movies; *however,* I changed my mind." That's a different context. Communicating about yourself is *one* thing, but when you are communicating about someone else's thoughts, ideas and opinions (especially a prospect's!) you want to be very sensitive to those words.

The key here, once again, is to practice and role play, because there is a huge difference between intellectual understanding and actually integrating it into a real conversation. The words *but* and *however* are so deeply ingrained in our psyche. When practicing this, you will be amazed at how habitual those words are.

Without exaggeration, the one tool I have just shared with you, when applied and implemented properly, can completely change your level of communication and the results you get. You can turn around someone's opinion and point of view without any disagreement or friction. It will allow you to develop rapport at a level you may have never thought was possible.

ENROLLING VS. CONVINCING

We established that the main barrier to effective communication is that people don't ... what? If you're having trouble remembering, this should be a clue. The main barrier, as a rule, is that people don't **listen!** One of the best ways to be a better listener is to ask effective questions. If you want to be truly great at handling objections, you need to come from the perspective of asking more and better questions.

This may seem like a rather obvious distinction, but (notice I'm using the "B" word in regards to my *own* point) it brings up one of the most important distinctions I could possibly give you around handling objections: to be absolutely unstoppable at handling objections, you must **give up the approach of trying to *"convince"* people.**

Why is that? When you are focused on convincing people, you're focused on what you're going to *tell* them. "I'm going to give him or her a million and a half reasons why, and I'm going to show him exactly why he needs to..." etc. You're focused on talking. How often have you heard people say: *"I did a really good job of convincing her, but she just didn't budge,"* or *"I spent hours convincing the guy, but he just didn't seem to see things my way."*

Think about this. The word "convince" comes from the Latin roots *"com,"* which means "intention;" and *"vincere,"* which means, "to conquer." **The intention to conquer.** I don't know about you, but when I think about what I hope to gain from a conversation with someone, I am often looking to learn something, or I may want to be entertained, or I may even want to be challenged, but I am not looking to be conquered. Make sense?

So don't look to conquer people in conversations. Instead, you want to focus on **enrolling** your prospect. When you convince someone, you are getting them to do something for *your* reasons; but when you enroll someone, you get them to do it for *their* reasons.

You're getting her to look inside and consider new possibilities and how those possibilities might work. You're not just giving her more reasons; you're getting her on board, ultimately to a point where she would want to do it **with or without you** (as Bono would say).

The goal is to take on what I refer to as an *"enrolling way of being."* **Please let that swim around in your mind for a few moments.** In other words, become someone who is constantly asking questions, challenging people to reevaluate, and encouraging them to contemplate how they operate or look at things. Become extremely aware and tuned in to what might be going on in the mind of the other person—don't just *tell* them why they *should* think or feel a certain way.

One of Webster's definitions of enrollment is: *"To accept as a member."* Think about that. When you are enrolling someone into an idea, you are not just handing them the idea; you are getting them to accept the idea as *their own.* It literally belongs to them.

Be someone who asks a lot of questions!

And would you like to know the best way to introduce a question? This one distinction can be the difference that determines whether or not you get an answer. The best way to begin asking questions is to get *permission to ask* first. You say, *"Can I ask you a question?"* or, *"Do you mind if I ask you a few brief questions?"* or something along those lines.

First of all, it confirms for you that you really do have permission. Your prospect may not be ready to start answering questions. Next, and perhaps more importantly, it draws more attention to the question you're about to ask.

You can also simply let the prospect know or *announce* you're about to ask her a question by saying: **"Let me ask you a question"** or simply, **"Question:"** and then ask your question. This lays out the red carpet for what you're about to ask and draws more attention to it as well.

RESPONDING POSITIVELY OUT LOUD

Speaking of questions, I've got one for you—a big one. It is related to the previous chapter. Now that you have this new way of mentally responding to objections when they are handed to you, such as thinking statements like *"awesome,"* or, *"excellent!"*... **What if you actually did that out loud?**

Just take that in for a moment.

What if, every time someone handed you an objection, you literally gave a positive response and said, *"Excellent,"* or, *"Thank you,"* or, *"Awesome,"* **out loud?** Right now you may be saying, "Alright, I was with him up until now, but this guy has just gone over the deep end." Just hang in there.

Please just think about it and be open.

First of all, would that be empowering for *you* to actually hear yourself saying that? Just for your level of confidence and your state of mind?

But moreover, what do you think it would do to the mind of your prospect? Do you think it could possibly interrupt your *prospect's* pattern of thought—throw him a curve ball, make him stop and actually think for a moment? Do you think you could possibly separate yourself from the overwhelming majority of your competition right there? Do you think, on some level, your prospect would be at least a little bit impressed with how his rejection didn't even faze you?

When someone hands you an objection or says "no," what kind of response do they usually expect? Usually they expect one of two responses—either intimidation or aggression. Either you're going to be intimidated and shy away from the objection and say things like, *"Oh, okay,"* or, *"Oh, I'm sorry, I didn't mean to offend you... I'll get back to you..."* or something like that; *or* you're going to attack it and just jump all over them and say, *"Yeah, but don't you see...!"* or, *"I know you think that's how it is, but let me show you how it really is...!"* etc.

What if:

What if, after a prospect just gave you their hardest objection—really gave you their best—instead of reacting with one of the responses just described, you looked them right in the eyes (if in person) and with conviction and sincerity said: *"Awesome! I'm more excited now than before you said that. I understand why you feel that way, and can I ask you a few brief but very important questions?"*

What if you really meant it when you said it, and it really came through? How powerful would that be?

"Awesome! I understand exactly how you feel *and* can I ask you a question?"

When you say the word *"awesome,"* it doesn't have to be hyped up; it doesn't even have to be the word awesome. It can be *"excellent,"* or, *"that's great,"* or, *"thank you,"* or, *"perfect,"* or your own word. The point is that you are responding positively and optimistically, directly in the face of rejection, and doing it in a way that is natural for you. I want you to think about the paradigm shift we are creating here.

Have you ever been the *prospect* in a conversation like that? Where *you* were dealing with a salesperson, or anyone for that matter, and when you tried to shoo them away with a few objections, they made it absolutely clear they were not fazed in the least? Where they were, in fact, actually having fun with it, and just kept coming back and asking you questions in a polite, professional and courteous manner?

At one point you start to say to yourself: *"Okay, here we go."* You know you're in a conversation with a real pro. And when you finish doing business with someone like that, how do you usually feel? You feel great don't you? Very often, you're thankful for their persistence.

So please review the below response once again:

"Awesome! I understand exactly how you feel, and can I ask you a question?"

You should see the transformation my audiences go through at live events with this one statement! It has been known to singlehandedly change sales careers. Not the words themselves, but the shift in paradigm and in the attitude that inherently come along with this response.

Just as I had you practice and reinforce the initial positive responses internally in the previous chapter, I'd like you to practice and reinforce this. Go through the list of objections that are predominant for you and practice responding with this out loud. Once again, you can find someone to practice and role-play with.

And once again, if you are a veteran of your industry, this applies to you in particular!

For example:

There isn't enough money in our budget.

"Awesome! I understand exactly how you feel, and can I ask you a question?"

I am just not interested right now.

"Excellent! I understand exactly how you feel, and can I ask you a question?"

Please send me out some information, and if I'm interested, I'll get back to you.

"Thank you! I understand why you'd make that request, and can I ask you a question?"

Your fee is too high. I just spoke with XYZ competitor who is 10% less expensive.

"Perfect! I understand that's a concern, and can I ask you a question?"

I need to speak with_____before I do anything.

"Okay! I understand exactly how you feel, and let me ask you a question."

I don't feel like getting into this right now.

"Message received loud and clear! I understand exactly how you're feeling right now, and let me ask you a question."

You can apply this to virtually any objection or concern the prospect has to offer you. For this to be as effective and natural as possible, I encourage you to treat the above response as a **template.** In other words, use the basic principle and structure, but **insert whatever words work best for you.**

For example, you can substitute *"awesome"* with, *"thank you,"* or you can substitute, *"I understand exactly how you feel,"* with, *"I hear you loud and* clear." *"Can I ask you a question?"* can be substituted with, *"May I just ask you a few brief but really important questions?"*

The following are some sample responses using the same template, but with different words:

"Thank you for letting me know where you stand on this! In your shoes, I think I would feel the exact same way, and can I get your opinion on something?"

"Got it! You make a very valid point. I can see where you're coming from; and can I ask you an important question about that?"

"Excellent! I was hoping you would say that, because it shows me that you're really engaged here, and I'm curious—can I ask you a question?"

Get into the habit of responding to objections this way, in an upbeat and emphatic manner, and watch how it transforms your career.

SPECIFIC QUESTIONS TO ASK

Now, you may be saying to yourself: "That's great. But what questions do I ask?

First of all, **just ask any question,** *and you'll be much better off than if you simply talk too much,* which is what most sales "professionals" do! This, of course, assumes they're appropriate questions. After empathizing with your prospect and getting permission to ask a question, asking what she was thinking when she put that outfit on or what he has against using deodorant is clearly not ideal.

But I would like to share some specific questions I have found to be extremely effective.

Questions like these are the core foundation for being an effective objection-handler. The key is that you must ask them in a way that is normal and natural for you. These are vitally important.

The first is what I call the *"default"* or the *"go-to"* question, because it is a question you can ask at any point in the dialogue, and it is a great way to interrupt the pattern of conversation if you feel it is starting to take a bad turn or if you are starting to feel a bit lost about where to go in the conversation. It is a question that almost every prospect will listen to and be willing to answer.

Traditionally it is taught as a question used to qualify your prospect, but I am here to tell you that you can and should use it when having a closing conversation or handling objections as well. The question is:

"What is most important to you regarding____?"

For example:

"What is most important to you regarding the home you are looking to buy?"

"What's most important to you regarding the growth of your sales force and seeing them succeed at the highest level?"

"What is most important to you regarding the computer system you want for this office?"

"What is most important to you regarding the financial advisor you choose to work with?"

"What is most important to you regarding the insurance policy you obtain for yourself and your family?"

"What is most important to you regarding the new position we find for you?"

Some other ways you can word this question, which have essentially the same meaning, are:

"What's most important here?"

"What is the single most important thing...?"

"What matters most...?"

"What are you really looking to get out of...?"

"Why did you consider doing this in the first place?"

"Out of all of your considerations, what is top priority here?"

"Out of everything we have been discussing here, what is the one thing you simply cannot do without?"

When asking these questions, I encourage you to do so in a ***"let's get down to the heart of the matter"*** or ***"just level with me"*** tone of voice.

It will show that you are being real, not salesy, and that you just want to get to the point. This can be extremely refreshing for a prospect. Oftentimes it will immediately change the tone, tempo and pace of the conversation, while simultaneously putting you in control. This is very often when the prospect will say to herself, *"Okay, now this person is speaking my language,"* or something to that effect.

Once the prospect gives you his answer, you can begin to sell from that perspective, if you have not been doing so already. If you actually answered this question when qualifying your prospect earlier (which I would recommend), you may already know the answer, and you can simply say something to the effect of:

"When we spoke earlier, you told me that _____ was hands-down the most important consideration here. Is that indeed the case?"

If they answer, *"yes"* to that question, you move forward and sell from that perspective. If they say "no," then it's a good thing you asked; and it's also time to find out the right answer! I find that it is a good idea to re-ask the question, even if you have asked previously, because oftentimes it is when you ask again, after the sleeves have been rolled up and you're getting down to brass tacks, that you get the real answer.

Next, you want to *identify the reason(s) behind the objection.* You uncover your prospect's "why:"

"Why do you feel that way?"
"I know you have a reason for saying that. Do you mind if I ask what it is?"
"Can I ask what makes you feel that way?"

Once you've been handed an objection and hopefully have uncovered the reasons behind it, *you make it a final objection.* You clarify that this is the big one, the real issue, the sticking point:

"If we could get past this as an issue, would you feel more comfortable moving ahead?"

"If this were not a concern, would we be in a position to go to the next step?"

"Is this a deal-stopper?"

Or something to this effect. You want to make sure you ask these questions in a very informal "by-the-way" manner, because questions such as these can be considered "old school" and some of your prospects might have heard them before. But make no mistake! They are a *great* way to gauge how significant a particular objection is, and they are a fantastic way to move the conversation forward.

If the prospect answers with a *"yes,"* then you simply begin handling the objection—of course, using more questions than statements, as always. If the prospect answers *"no,"* then you respond with the question:

"There must be something else causing you to hesitate. Can I ask what it is?"

And you continue to search for the final or real objection. Once you've identified it, you address it and lay it to rest.

IT'S OKAY TO BE TRANSPARENT

This brings me to another very important point. Is it a bad thing if your prospect knows that you are looking to help her come to a decision and move forward? Is it bad if your prospect fully understands that your intention is to create a transaction and do business?

So many entrepreneurs hesitate to ask questions like the ones above because they are afraid their prospect will know what they're up to or think they are trying to "close" them, like it's a bad thing. I've got news for you that could make that whole idea much easier to deal with: **They already know this about you!**

They already realize you are not there solely on a mission of mercy. You did not walk in with a red-cross band wrapped around your arm. You are a businessperson and you have come with a purpose—to provide a product or service that matches or exceeds the value of any money they are going to give you. And make no mistake; they are going to give you their money!

If, for whatever reason, they should have an issue with that, (which, when you put aside your own internal fears and perceptions, you will find is much less common than you would think), then it is your job to call them out on it in a professional and courteous way. For example, when we are coming to the moment of decision and I am attempting to move the conversation along, the prospect might throw up barriers and say something along the lines of, *"Look, I know what you're doing here. You want the business. Don't think I don't know what you're doing,"* or *"Listen, I've been doing this for XX years and I see exactly where you're going here"*— as if they've found me out or I owe them an apology. I will usually respond with something along the lines of:

"Yes, and—your point is?"
"Right, and ah—so?"

Or one I love is:

"Well, I'm glad you do. If you didn't, I'd be a bit concerned. And let me ask you a question: would you want to let that get in the way of being able to benefit from what we're talking about here?"

This reflects my philosophy more than simply being an objection-handling "technique."

A good way to address the objection itself is what I call the "pain/pleasure" approach. The foundational principles of this approach and how they relate to influencing your prospect's decisions are outlined in Chapter 1 on conditioning your mind. It is very simple. You stir up pain or dissatisfaction in the mind of the prospect regarding her current situation, and then you give her the opportunity to heal and, ultimately, to replace that pain with the pleasure of your solution instead.

How badly someone is bleeding will dictate how quickly they get to the hospital.

For example:

Is your current _____ giving you everything you want in that area? There must be a reason you are having this conversation with me.

Have you ever considered the fact that your current _____ doesn't provide you with _____?

How do you feel about the fact that when it comes to _____ , your current is underperforming the industry average/doesn't even come close to what we're offering?

Have you ever been dissatisfied with your current _____? What about it in particular?

Have you considered the cost that not addressing this topic up until now has had on your life/business?

What about _____ isn't good enough yet?

If it were up to you, what would you most like to improve about _____?

How could _____ be performing better?

In your opinion, what has that been costing you over the last XX years?

If you continue to operate/use/live in/deal with _____ and the limitations we have identified here, what could that mean to you long term?

(This is also known as "future pacing"—creating the future in advance.)

Is that really how you want go through the next XX years?"

Do you get the idea? As you can see, there are a lot of possibilities for questions there. These are great questions to begin asking after you have asked: "What is most important to you regarding...?" as described above. Asking something along the lines of: *"What is going well,"* or *"What are you pleased with in regards to your current vendor?"* are good types of questions to ask before unleashing the pain-inducing questions, because they can soften the prospect up and create credibility before you go in to stir up the pain. But stir up the pain you must!

In stirring up the pain, using tie downs can be effective at truly bringing it home:

"What's the real cost there?"
"How does that make you feel?"
"Is that acceptable?"

I encourage you to create some of your own. Once you have stirred up a "sufficient" amount of pain and dissatisfaction—and I put "sufficient" in quotations, because that is relevant to the conversation and the prospect—you can then redirect the dialogue towards all of the pleasure and benefits the prospect will experience by working with you instead.

A great way to begin those redirecting questions is by saying:

"What if, instead, you could...?"

Or:

"What would happen if...?"
"Are you open to the possibility of...?"
"What if, instead, you:

- *Could have the advantage of using _____?*
- *Could have access to _____ 24/7, at no extra fee?*
- *Could live in a neighborhood that has a far superior _____?*
- *Had a system that not only did _____, but did _____ as well?*
- *Never had to worry about _____ again?*
- *Were working with someone moving forward who would handle that for you and would keep you abreast of progress every step of the way?*
- *Knew, moving forward, there would be no last minute fees that you were not previously told about?*
- *Could work a job that offered you _____ and _____ as well at an even higher salary?*

- *Had a personal representative who handled all of your concerns and who knew you by name, instead of calling up an 800-number which kept you on hold for ten minutes every time you called?*
- *Received an email at the end of every business day letting you know exactly the status and balance of your account, instead of waiting for a monthly statement in the mail?*
- *Had an advisor who was on the phone with you immediately in the event of any significant changes with your position/investment?*

As you can see, there are an endless number of examples with these questions. Once again, I encourage you to modify these or create some questions of your own tailored to your niche. Would it be worth putting aside ten minutes to create some questions that could change the direction of your career? I certainly hope so!

Next is what I call *"The Reverse."* When used effectively, this is an *incredibly* powerful tool. The reverse refers to when you are speaking in statements, not questions. As important and powerful as the effective use of questions is, and you'll hear me talk about that all day long, there are also times when you will simply need to speak and make statements.

The reverse is best used when responding emphatically to an objection the prospect has just handed you, or you can use it to follow up the pain-inducing questions I laid out earlier. After those questions have been asked, the "soil has been tilled," so to speak. In other words, the prospect's defenses have been taken down and he is more open to receive.

You're basically taking the prospect's objection and turning it right around on him, using it as the exact reason he needs to go ahead with what you are suggesting. You do this by using the phrase:

"That's *exactly* why you should_____."

When you do this effectively, you can totally change the paradigm of the conversation with one statement. The key to this is to have a good reason (or reasons) prepared to back it up. And notice I italicized the word *"exactly"* for added emphasis, because this is the word you want to emphasize when making this statement. Examples:

"I understand you don't have the time. And that's **exactly** why you need to do this *now*: because you are never going to have the perfect amount of time. Your schedule is going to be just as busy six weeks from now, if not busier. And I'm sure you'd agree, there's rarely if ever a perfect time to do anything. Agreed?"

"I understand you are already working with someone else right now. And that's **exactly** why we should meet. Because I am not looking to disrupt any relationships you currently have. I am simply looking to introduce myself, give you a fresh perspective, and educate you about some additional options. And I'm sure you'd agree, with something as important as this, having a fresh perspective could be very helpful, whether or not you and I ever work together. Make sense? Great. So when would you like to meet?"

"I respect the fact that you want to hold off. And that's **exactly** why you should take action right now. Because you've already taken six months to make a decision regarding this critical topic and it still hasn't happened. Continuing to delay and procrastinate could move you deeper down the same rabbit hole, and you could miss a critical time in the market right now if you don't take action. Fair enough?"

Or after the pain/dissatisfaction-inducing questions:

"Understanding that_____is clearly an issue for you, that is *exactly* why you should work with us. And I say that because ..."

And then give your reasons to justify it!

Next—and you can do this at any point of the conversation—*turn the objection into a question:*

"Understanding you are concerned about *[objection]*, isn't the real question here: how can you have *[primary benefit]*?"

Some examples of this:

"Understanding that the *fee* is a concern to you right now, isn't the real question here: how can you net the best possible *bottom line profit* on the sale of your home?"

"I understand that we are *more expensive* than XYZ, and based on what you and I have already discussed, wouldn't you agree that what's really most important here is: *will this machine do what you said you needed it to do,* and do it reliably for the next five years without having to buy a new one?"

"I understand you want to do some more *research*, and wouldn't you agree that the several hours of research you may or may not do couldn't possibly compare to the *six years of experience* I have in this particular area?"

Using the above approach, of course, assumes that you have effectively qualified your prospect up front and you know what their core or "hot button" values are; and thus you also know their primary benefit. This is from where you derive the *primary benefit* part of that question.

And by the way, if you do not know the primary benefit or pain that is driving your prospect, **it is your job to find out**! Perhaps you need to re-read the chapter on qualifying your prospect again.

CONCLUSION

In closing, I have one thing to say about the skill of objection handling.

Master how to do it and, I promise, your life will never be the same! You will walk upon this earth with a feeling of confidence that very few ever know— like a true Sales Samurai!

REVIEW:

- You want to align with your prospect by *empathizing* with his or her point of view. No one wants to be made to feel wrong.
- The two words you want to avoid if at all possible when addressing a prospect's concerns are the words *"but"* and *"however."* These two words destroy rapport and kill sales. You want to replace them with the word *"and."*
- You want to focus on *enrolling* your prospect into doing business with you through the effective use of questions instead of convincing her through statements.
- You want him to take action for *his* reasons, not yours.

- The best way to begin to ask questions is to get *permission to ask*, or *announce that you're about to ask* first. This directs more attention to the question(s) you are about to ask and confirms you do in fact have permission.
- There are many different kinds of questions you can ask.
- Stirring up pain in the mind of the prospect as to what about his current situation is not satisfactory, then healing and replacing that pain with the pleasure of working with you, can be extremely effective.
- The "reverse" with the strategic and powerful use of the phrase *"That is exactly why..."* can be extremely effective as well.

7

DEFENDING YOUR FEE

GETTING PAID WHAT YOU'RE WORTH

THE THREE MAIN AREAS YOU MUST ADDRESS

One vital aspect of creating success, which I see so many entrepreneurs struggle with, is getting paid what they are worth—charging top dollar for their product or service and defending their fee. Not only does this struggle steal money from the businessman or woman, but it also leaves one feeling disempowered. It conjures up feelings of inadequacy—of not feeling worthy or deserving—as if you sold yourself short (which you did). You may feel like a fraud or think the prospect can see right through the story you are attempting to tell. Struggling with this aspect of your professional life is debilitating and has single-handedly halted the flowering of many, many potentially great careers.

To master this part of your sales game, there are three primary areas you must address and ultimately master:

1. **How you live your *own* life in regards to spending money and paying professional fees**
2. **Your professional identity**
3. **Your selling skills**

Master these three areas and you will empower yourself beyond belief! You will also open the door to becoming one of the highest paid individuals in your industry. So let's take a look at all three.

HOW YOU LIVE YOUR OWN LIFE IN REGARDS TO MONEY

Question: **How do you approach the issues of price or fee when it comes to your *own* money?** Do you tend to focus on price first or even price only, always looking to get the biggest discount with consideration for everything else as secondary or as non-existent? How do you live your *own* life regarding this?

When it comes time to spend your own money or make buying decisions, how to you handle this process? How heavily do you weigh the factor of price or fee? Are you what I call a *"habitual tightwad?"* I encourage you to take a rigorous personal inventory of yourself in this area. This is absolutely critical.

If you had to look at the world in terms of either/or, would you rather purchase something that saves you *a lot* of money but is of inferior quality, or would you rather pay *significantly* more but know you're getting something that is superior? Is price the *very first* thing you tend to look at and worry about before everything else?

I encourage you to look at this in terms of extremes to help make this clearer. Given the choice, what would you prefer? Answer this from a gut level—not who you think you *should* be or want to be—but from a place of who you really are. Take a look at how you actually think and act in those situations.

Important: Attempting to recommend, let alone persuade, someone else to do something or make a decision that you clearly would not follow through with yourself can be extremely difficult, if not impossible. Think about the contradiction there. You're living a lie! You don't have any mental legs to stand on, and your subconscious knows it.

Money is such an emotionally charged issue for so many of your prospects. Memorizing a bunch of closes to address their objections when they come up simply is not enough. Your levels of belief and conviction regarding this topic *must* be deep. They must be strong enough to push through the hesitation and fear your prospects feel when they object to your fee, price or commission. **Words alone just won't cut it.**

I want to stress something that is very important here. I realize when making virtually *any* buying decision, there are numerous factors you will consider. Price or cost is usually only one of them. I understand you don't live in a one-dimensional universe. But here's the challenge: most people walk around believing they take all factors into consideration simultaneously and that, with a balanced perspective, they make the most intelligent choices.

That's a great concept. But I will tell you what my study and analysis of human behavior over the years has shown me. **When making a buying decision, your mind tends to habitually go towards *one* of these factors first—*consistently!*** There is a consistent, habitual pattern your mind plays out. It could have developed due to your upbringing or conditioning; an experience you had when you were a child; a movie or television show you once saw; something you learned in school; or an experience you had when you were a "bigger child," also known as an adult.

The most important thing to understand for the purpose of this discussion is *it doesn't matter where it came from!* I am not looking to have you psychoanalyze yourself here. In this discussion, I am simply interested in identifying whether or not you display this habitual pattern—and if so, helping you to get rid of it.

Because if you do react this way, always worrying about price and how much something is going to cost first and foremost, *yes, even with a limited budget*, mastering your ability to address the price or fee issue with difficult prospects is going to be *extremely* challenging. Good luck with that one.

Imagine if I was going out every day telling people I met professionally to stay away from alcohol, and then each night I drank a six-pack. Imagine if I was looking to sell people on the idea of getting consistent exercise and working out regularly, and I hadn't been in the gym or gotten exercise myself for over a year. Think about how ridiculous that would be.

Well, that is what's happening *every time* you attempt to persuade someone to pay top dollar or a full service fee when you, yourself, avoid it like the plague! When I think about how much money and opportunity are left on the table as a result of this one blind spot, it astounds me.

Now, I want to stress something else that is also very important here. I'm not saying you should never look for good deals or be willing to negotiate. Of course you should! That's a part of life, and the person who doesn't do that is, in a way, stealing from himself as well. I encourage you to constantly get the best possible value for the best possible price.

What I am saying is this: if you let the singular concern of price or fee be the primary driving force in the purchase decisions you make, to the point where it blinds you from other considerations, not only will you cost yourself more money in the long-term as a consumer, but **you are going to have an extremely difficult time enrolling your prospects and your clients into paying top dollar** for whatever you are offering.

Consider the metaphor that your presentation is a car ride that is going along smoothly on a freshly paved road, until you attempt to persuade someone into doing something that you yourself do not really believe in or practice. The freshly paved road turns into an old, beaten up street made of cobblestone with potholes and ripped up cement. That is the turbulence and conflict your mind is going through when you attempt this exhausting feat.

I have a brief exercise for you. I'd like you to search your memory banks and recall how you have handled the following buying decisions in the past. This could be from years ago, or just the other day:

- The purchase, sale or renting of your home and the real estate agent(s) you worked with.
- The path you took and the loan officer you hired in finding a mortgage.

- The office equipment and technology you purchased for your home or office (if appropriate).
- Your car(s).
- Your clothing.
- The attorney(s) you've worked with.
- The financial advisor(s) you've worked with.
- Your CPA.
- Your gardener.
- Your dry cleaning.
- Grocery shopping.
- The restaurants you go to, and how you order.
- Your furniture.
- Your home entertainment system.
- The presents you tend to buy for people.
- How you deal with friends and family around lending and borrowing money.
- Insurance or lack thereof.

I want you to take a look at how you approached making these decisions—*especially* if you were managing a limited budget and paying for superior quality would have made a difference in your liquidity—at least in the short term. I don't want you to judge or demean yourself in any way about any of this, and if you don't want to share the results of this exercise with another living soul, that is fine. This is not about what is right or wrong, or what makes you a better or a lesser person. This is about what will serve and support you in being a more effective sales professional. When reviewing each of these decisions, ask yourself the following questions:

1. What was the *very first thing* my mind instinctively considered when looking at this?
   - Price (fee)
   - Quality
   - Utility

- Long-term value
- Convenience
- The level of service I'd be receiving
- Follow-through
- The individual/organization I'm dealing with

2. When I considered this decision, **how was I feeling?** Was I worried that I wouldn't have enough money for what I wanted, or was I confident that I'd be able to find something good within my budget? Was I coming from a place of **abundance** or **scarcity?**

3. Was I interested in getting a deal that was good for everyone, or screwing the other party out of as much money as possible so I could save more?

4. **Did I enjoy the fact that the person selling it to me would be compensated, or did I resent it?**

5. Was I willing to give the salesperson or representative a chance and was I willing to listen to what she had to say, or did I immediately write her off because she had something to sell me?

6. Even though I may not have had any expertise in that area, did I feel that I would have been better off doing it myself?

Take a serious look at these questions—once again without any judgment.

What do they reveal to you?

If you believe you are already *completely self-actualized* in this area and don't have any limiting thought patterns, which I have found to be the *extreme* exception, then congratulations. All you need to do is master your professional identity and your selling skills, and you are home free. But if you are like the majority of people, you probably observed that **as the prospect, you could be just as cheap, just as difficult, just as closed-minded, and just as stubborn on price as the next person.** If this is the case, then please believe me when I say that it would serve you to do some work on yourself in this area—and thank goodness you are reading this! And don't fret. It's not uncommon, and the solution is not as complex as you might think.

So what is the solution? Very simply this: From this point forward, make a total commitment to yourself to look first at *quality, utility,* and things like the *long- term intrinsic value* or the *level of service* you are receiving. Let these be your primary driving factors, because they are, in fact, what you are enrolling your prospects into looking at and paying for. And be *happy* that the salesperson is making money as a result of working with you. Look to be a part of transactions where everyone makes out well, not just you—*yes, even as the consumer!*

Once you have done that, *then* look for the best possible price and what fits into your budget. At the end of the day, if it turns out something just isn't in your budget and you can't afford it, then as Yogi Berra the famous baseball player and manager used to say, *"It is what it is."* At least you've come to that decision as an intelligent consumer, not as a fear-driven bottom feeder.

Watch how this transforms your level of conviction with your own prospects!

To make this even more tangible for you, I'd like you to recall some times when you were driven by price or cost exclusively and you ended up paying a bigger price for it down the line. Conversely, I'd like you to think about some times when you made the decision to pay more for higher quality and were ultimately thankful and pleased that you had.

One example I mentioned briefly in chapter four involved a decision I made years ago regarding my taxes. It was the first year I was working as a 1099 independent contractor, which is completely different from being paid on a W2 basis. If managed properly, the tax advantages and write offs for an independent contractor can be tremendous—and rightfully so. You are investing more into your business and taking on a lot more responsibility.

I had a decent year that year and decided to go to a large household name, factory-type of taxation service (which shall remain nameless) that had a storefront in my neighborhood. This was despite the fact that friends of mine had recommended various personal accountants who were "specialists" and experts at working with people in my situation. I quickly dismissed those recommendations because I noticed that the "specialists" charged significantly more than the larger firms, and some even worked on a monthly retainer and were looking for a long-term relationship. What a concept!

After sitting in a waiting room with about ten other people, I was handed off to the first available accountant. The gentleman who helped me was pleasant enough, but the bottom line is that he didn't understand my situation and had no clue as to how to maximize my expenses and expenditures. He ran me though a standardized template he had been given by the company, which he went through with everyone he met, most of whom were W2 employees!

At a certain point during the consultation, I started to realize he didn't really grasp what I was doing and wasn't interested in going too deeply into the particulars. He just wanted to get the job done. But my thinking was, "Hey, the guy's a professional; they've got him doing this for a reason. How bad could it be?" Those are what we call *famous last words*.

I also happened to have a busy week scheduled with a lot of other things going on and a conference call appointment later in the day, etc... Perhaps you know what I'm talking about. A part of me just wanted to get it over with as well.

The bottom line is, as a result of going that route and saving a few hundred dollars in the initial consultation, I figured out that I literally left close to **$30,000** on the table that year that should have been mine. I'm not talking about aggressive or creative accounting; I'm talking about simply knowing the score and the right way to do things!

There is often a huge price paid as a result of thinking about price first. I know—the irony. The very next year I hired a specialist who charged a much higher fee, but who did a tremendous job and saved me tens of thousands of dollars, which I would have lost had I been working with a factory, cookie-cutter, discount-type accounting service. That is just one example.

A less dramatic example that comes to mind is the dry cleaner I use. I live in New York City where things are already more expensive overall, and I go to a specific dry cleaner where I pay $6.00 per shirt, when the average in the city is $4.00. That's a 50% differential! Trust me, it adds up.

But I do it because they hand press every shirt individually. Not only do the shirts come out looking sharper overall, but the cleaner hand presses my collars as well. With all of the public speaking I do, I can't afford to have my collars even a little bent or crooked. It would affect my audiences' first impression immediately.

The thought of losing future speaking engagements or possible consulting relationships because I wasn't willing to spend an extra $2.00 on having my shirt hand pressed is ridiculous. But there are other consumers out there who would not be willing to pay the $6.00 because their primary driving force is price; they just want to get the cheapest price in the moment. And we've all seen the guy in the office with the crooked collar.

I have more examples I could give, but I trust you get the point. So, what are some examples that come to mind for *you* personally? I encourage you to take a few minutes and write some of those down.

Please take a few minutes and write down some examples of money lost by cutting corners and money saved by going with quality first.

Are you getting some clarity from this? **The way you show up in your own life is going to spill over into the way you present to and communicate with your prospects**—whether you consciously realize it or not.

Now consider this: what if you had your prospects answer the same kinds of questions you've been answering here—in a way that was a natural part of the conversation and that took them away from price as a concern— would that be helpful? Would that make it easier to deal with them on the topic of price and fee? Of course it would! We're going to take a look at that in a moment. But first, there is something else you must consider. And that is:

YOUR IDENTITY AS A PROFESSIONAL

Do you see yourself ("your-self," think about that) as a full-service, top-shelf individual? Are you the type of person who warrants and deserves the full boat—the high-end fee? Are you someone who is comfortable dealing with selling the high-end product and getting paid for it? When it comes to business, as Pete Townsend of *The Who* once wrote, "**Who are you?**"

This topic inevitably leads us to a discussion about your belief systems, because ultimately it is your beliefs that make up your self-concept and your perception of who you are. In the chapter titled "Your Beliefs: The Pain/Pleasure Navigator," I talk about this critical topic in much more detail. I recommend you read that before going through this if you have not done so already. If you've purchased this chapter as a separate e-book online, I strongly urge you to buy the chapter on belief systems, or the entire book for that matter.

When presenting to prospects, you are constantly put in situations where you need to justify or defend your fee. When it comes time to discuss price or fee with your prospect, do you feel your product or service is worth it—and not a penny less—*regardless of any complaints the prospect may have or whomever else they've spoken to or whatever other quote they say they've been given?*

This is the key. We're going beyond words and to your level of **belief—your self-concept.** As the saying goes, *"It's not what you say, it's how you say it."* Picture someone who has their shoulders slumped, head held low, looking down and avoiding eye contact with you while saying in a bland monotone voice at a volume you can barely hear: *"I am so excited right now."* You know they don't really mean it! They're not connected to what they are saying.

So recall how you *feel* in the moment you're defending your fee and justifying what you charge. Wherever you may be on that scale of conviction, I have found that the following writing exercise can be incredibly helpful in raising that level. Please take a few minutes and write down every answer you can come up with to complete the following two sentences. Using a separate piece of paper or a computer may not be a bad idea:

"The fee I charge for my service is only a fraction of the value I bring to the table. My clients are getting off cheap. I deserve every penny I earn and more because:"

_____

_____

_____

_____

_____

_____

_____

_____

_____

"My product is worth every penny I am asking for and more because:"

_____

_____

_____

_____

_____

_____

_____

_____

_____

Shouldn't you be crystal clear on your answers to these questions before going out and presenting to even one prospect? Of course! This is truly fundamental.

If you have been shaky on this, then remember that was in the past. The good news is that going forward from this moment on, you never need to be unclear in this area again. A lot of the work I do with my personal coaching and consulting clients, both new and seasoned, revolves around this specific topic. Some of the transformation I have seen and been a part of in this area has been jaw dropping. If you are already feeling powerful in this area, then continue on and challenge yourself to see how much better you can be.

I encourage you to consistently read through and review the answers above. Think about and meditate on them before speaking with prospects. You might want to create some affirmations or declarations that you repeat to yourself constantly about these answers. It is incredibly powerful! I can tell you that practice made a huge difference in my own life.

I also want you to know that I have experience with this topic first hand. I worked as a full-service financial advisor on Wall Street for close to seven years. "Full-service" means full service was given and full-service fees were charged.

The advent of the Internet put that to the test for many people. All of a sudden you had investors who had quick, easy access to better research. You also had discount brokers like Charles Schwab, T. Rowe Price and Ameritrade popping up all over the place, online trading, etc.

But what many investors did not realize was that there were still significant differences between working with a discount cut-rate broker and a committed, full-service financial advisor. For example, while the investor could now access research online, it very often paled in comparison with the research and information that many full-service, wire-house firms were offering. There was a different depth of understanding and detail.

In addition, when there was a sudden fluctuation in the market or in a position that an investor was holding onto, a full-service advisor would be on the phone with the client immediately, letting her know what was happening and giving strategic advice on how to react to protect her assets and hedge her risk.

The discount firms didn't even contact the client. Why? Because they were discount firms! They weren't being paid for that level of service. You had investors who took a bath on some of their stocks and didn't even know until they went online after the close or read the newspaper the next day.

But regardless, especially in the beginning, the objection *"your commissions are too high,"* started popping up all over the place when it had almost never come up before. This became a challenge for many full-service advisors—*but not for all.* There were and still are *many* full-service advisors who flourish by charging the full-service fees they always have—and justifiably so.

Because when your professional identity and your conviction come through, and when you communicate in that fashion, people are still willing—and in my opinion, will always be willing—to pay top dollar for service (and product) that deserves it.

That is just one example from my own experience. I have also done a lot of consulting and coaching work in the real estate, mortgage, asset management, insurance, office solutions, telecom, computer industries and more, and I see this issue coming up in some way, shape or form in every industry, across the board.

At the end of the day, this requires a very clear decision. It requires you to make the decision to know you and your product/service are worth *every penny* you are asking for and more; that your prospect is getting off cheap; that you are worthy; and that great things are headed your way, because you deserve them. With that mindset in place, what could possibly stop you?

And finally:

YOUR SELLING SKILLS ON THIS TOPIC

As always, the most important distinction to make on your selling skills in this area is the same distinction I urge you to make with any selling skill, and that is to **make sure you are asking a lot of effective questions and listening more than you are speaking.** This is first and foremost, and comes before *anything* else.

With that in place, remember that the best time to handle an objection is *before* it comes up. If you think price/fee may come up as an objection, then your job is to preempt it. The concept of the "pre-frame" I mentioned in Chapter 4, "Qualifying Your Prospect With Direction And Purpose," comes to mind here. You want to point out and even tout the fact that you are more expensive than your competition (if this is the case) as one of the things that sets you apart. Have it be part of your identity. For example, to use an old but effective statement: *"We are the Rolls Royce of the industry."* These days, it would be the *"Apple"* or *"Bose"* of your industry. Speak as if you are in another league than your competition from the very beginning. Create a very strong pre-frame or predisposition for your prospect up front.

If you have effectively qualified your prospect, given a great presentation, done a strong job of preempting the price objection, and confidently and assertively asked for the business, but despite all this, the issue of price or fee still comes up, there are several things you can do. I would first like to credit two people in particular for a lot of my knowledge in this area: Brian Tracy and Zig Ziglar. These men have taught me a lot about how to address this critical topic.

First of all, be sure to apply the principles I share in the chapters titled "Turning Objections Into Transactions!" Integrate these into anything you learn here. Those principles are incredibly powerful and I encourage you to review those sections as often as possible. In addition, some things to say:

- "You are correct, our price/fee is higher than ABC competition, yet every year we sell millions of dollars worth of [your product/service] to some of the smartest consumers in the market. Would you like to know why?"
- "Yes, you are correct, our price/fee is higher than ABC competition, yet every year we outsell ABC by_____% (if that is true). Would you like to know why?"
- "Yes, you are correct, our price/fee is higher than ABC competition, yet every year our retention rate of existing customers is_____% higher than that of ABC. Would you like to know why?"
- "You are correct; our price/fee is higher than ABC competition. You see, years ago our company made a decision: we chose to offer

a higher quality [product/service] for a premium fee instead of offering an inferior version on the cheap. We decided it would be easier to explain price once to a satisfied customer than to apologize for poor quality indefinitely."

- "Would you agree that generally in life you get what you pay for?" *(And then ask them for specific examples!)*

When worded properly, this last rebuttal is a very powerful question to ask, because virtually everyone will answer yes to it. But notice I use the word "generally," because when put into absolutes, this statement isn't necessarily always true. For better or worse, you don't *always* get what you pay for. But most prospects can agree that as a rule, this statement is true in general.

But assuming it's been worded properly, one of the biggest mistakes most sales professionals make when asking this question is they get the answer and then leave it alone. Simply getting intellectual agreement from your prospect on this isn't enough. You don't just want people to agree with you intellectually, you want them to experience it on a gut, emotional level.

So be sure to give and to get examples. After getting permission from your prospect, give specific examples of when something like that happened to you.

And make it interesting. So I would give the example I mentioned previously about my tax service experience, or about the fact that I consistently receive compliments on "looking sharp" at speaking engagements, or past experiences I had years ago where I had to waste time in the morning re-ironing a shirt before appearing on stage, or a slew of other examples.

Once you've done that and you see that your prospect really gets it, then ask in a normal, conversational tone (not a "sales" tone):

"Have *you* ever had an experience like that yourself?" [*pause*] "What's one of yours?"

You will be amazed at how eager people are to talk about themselves or about times in their life when things have gone wrong, even when they understand exactly why you're asking the question and how it relates to your sales presentation. Let them talk about themselves and their experiences. If they hesitate or just aren't sure, you can say:

- "Just humor me on this. Give me *one* example."
- "If you *could* think of something, what would it be?"
- "What's one that really sticks out?"
- "Oh, come on (teasing). Everyone's had at least *one* experience like that."

If they get into a story of their own, you have now officially taken control of the conversation regarding the topic of price/fee. And once you've really gotten them connected to this answer, you end with:

"I'm sure you'd agree, good things are seldom cheap, and cheap things are seldom good."

And then pause briefly to let it sink in. When done effectively, this is *extremely* powerful.

Next is turning the price or fee objection into a question. Assuming you have qualified your prospect and know what his "hot buttons" or emotional pressure points are, and you have gotten a genuine answer to the question: *"What is most important to you in regards to this decision?"* you can then ask:

"Understanding that price/fee is a concern, isn't *the primary benefit* what's really most important here?" For example, "Understanding that price/fee is a concern, isn't...

- ...having a data storage platform you know you can rely on...
- ...the peace of mind that comes from knowing you got the best possible coverage for your family...
- ...the percentage increase in production you are seeing in your sales force...

- ...finding the right home/property in the area you want by the deadline you had mentioned...
- ...knowing you will be working with someone who will negotiate for you aggressively each and every time out...
- ...working with someone you know you can trust...
- ...getting a solid return without unnecessary risk...

... what's *really* most important here?"

And let your prospect answer!

If they answer *"no"* to a question structured this way, which is rare, simply ask the question, "Why not?" and let them shoulder the responsibility of the apparent contradiction. Allow them to bear the burden of justifying what they have just said. This is where a lot of the seeding and pre-frame work you did previously around *"self-concept consistency"* and *"meaning what you say"* can come back to support you in a big way. Make comparisons to other buying decisions where it would be foolish to even consider price as the only or primary concern. These are usually very important decisions:

"Would you say that what we're talking about here is an important decision? Of course.

What if, God forbid, you had to go in for a heart transplant tomorrow? Would it be safe to say that would be a fairly important decision in your life as well? Of course it would.

Well, I have a question. When it came time to pick the specialist who is going to open up your chest and decide your fate, are you going to look for the cheapest, lowest-priced, nickel-and-dime surgeon in the area? Of course not! You are going to look for the best, most highly regarded surgeon in the state, if not the entire country—regardless of price.

Because the decision is that important. Correct?

Well, why would you treat this decision with any less priority? Why would you look at it through the lens of price only, when there is clearly so much more to consider?"

Or:

"When you look for a formal dress/business suit, do you look at price only? Do you get all of your business clothing at Kmart? Of course not. Well then why would you treat this decision...?"

I'm sure there are many other examples you can come up with. The key is you want the examples to be extreme (yet relevant) so you can make the point powerfully. This is so effective!

CONCLUSION

As usual, from my perspective it is actually rather simple. When you represent your price or fee powerfully, you are living a different existence compared to the individual who constantly struggles with this. Not only do you make much more money, but you also feel empowered about what you do. Your self-concept and momentum explode through the roof!

As the founding fathers of the United States used to say when defending their independence against the Red Coats, *"Don't tread on me!"* You deserve every penny you are charging and more! Don't ever forget it.

REVIEW:

- Struggling with the issue of price or fee not only steals money from the pocket of the sales professional, but it leaves one feeling disempowered as well.
- To master this aspect of your sales game, there are three main areas you must address and ultimately master:
  1. How you live your *own* life in regards to money.
  2. Your professional identity.
  3. Your selling skills when presented with this as an issue.

- Attempting to recommend, let alone persuade, someone else to do something or make a decision that you clearly would not follow through with can be *extremely* difficult, if not impossible.
- You need to identify what factor(s) you consider *first and foremost* when making buying decisions for yourself.
- Your professional identity will inevitably come through when discussing the issue of fee, price and commission with your prospects. Simply memorizing a series of "closes" is not enough.
- In my opinion, people will always be willing to pay top dollar for products and services when they are presented effectively and powerfully and deserve it. There are plenty of specific turnarounds and rebuttals you can serve up to address this concern. I have made mention of the most important in this chapter.
- The best way to address the "commission" issue is to turn the conversation to the topic of value and put the prospect into the experience him/herself. Have her tell you stories of her own that make your point for you.
- Another effective approach is to make comparisons and analogies to other products or services where being cheap or thinking of price only would be ridiculous.
- Being able to defend price/fee effectively is one of the main things that separates top earners in any industry from the rest of the population.

8

THE POWER OF
GETTING CLEAR

IDENTIFYING WHAT YOU REALLY WANT, AND WHY

I have a question. What is the one thing, the one characteristic that separates the most successful people on the planet from the rest of the population? That's quite a question, yes?

Well, there are a lot of possible answers to that. I think most people would agree that truly successful people work hard, they stay consistent, they're committed, they're talented, they work *smart*, they get help when necessary, they stay the course, they're not stopped by setback, adversity or rejection, and they have a burning desire to be successful.

This indeed is all true. But I have another question. Is it possible that someone could possess all of those characteristics and *still* not achieve the success they are truly capable of? Of course it is! The proof? It happens all the time.

How many times have you seen someone who possesses some if not all of those characteristics, but they still don't seem to ever quite get it together? I can tell you that I've come across many people like that.

Calvin Coolidge once said, "Nothing is more common than unsuccessful men with talent." It's a bit sad. But it can also be an incredible learning lesson if you're paying attention. Because there is one critical element they are missing. One element, if not applied, can be the fatal flaw.

But when adhered to and leveraged properly, this can make all the difference in the world. This one element is absolutely necessary, absolutely critical for attaining true and consistent success in any endeavor. I don't care what niche or industry you're involved in. Without it, good luck. With it, you possess unbridled power beyond belief.

What I'm talking about very simply, is **clarity**. Being absolutely clear on your desired outcome or results. Knowing exactly what you want and perhaps even more importantly, why you want it.

Any truly effective program or seminar that I've ever been through on success or life mastery has had some portion dedicated to creating clarity and tapping into your "why." And when you're talking about succeeding in any branch of professional sales, it's even more important. Because to put it bluntly, very often you have to deal with a lot of nonsense and take a lot of crap to get to the top of the mountain.

Rejection, competition, people disappointing you and letting you down, saying one thing and doing another, skepticism, negativity, no guarantee of income, and more. So if you're not crystal clear on what you want to accomplish and why, you're going to have your hands full.

Now let's take a look at this. Why is clarity so important? It's important because it is a fundamental key to all life long success. Without it, your mind doesn't have a direction to move in. Without it, you're just flailing in the wind, shooting from the hip, at the whim of whatever happens to be surrounding you or in your mind at the present moment.

When you ask most people what they want, they tend to give general, even vague answers. They tend to say things like: "Well, I want to close more business; I want to make more money. I want a better relationship. I want to lose weight or get into better shape."

And all of those things are fine. But what's the problem with all of those answers? They're too general! I call this the "virus of vagueness."

How much money do you desire *exactly*? How much weight *precisely* do you want to lose, or gain and by when? What production or activity goals specifically are you committed to over the next one, three, five years?

One of the main reasons most people never accomplish what they truly want out of life is because they never get **clear** on what they truly want. To use a travel analogy, imagine if you were going to visit a family member who lived in Australia, for example. And you were excited and looking forward to seeing them.

And right before your trip someone asked you, well, where in Australia do they live? And you responded with the answer, "I don't know. Just Australia. I'm just going to get to the county and I'm sure I'll run into them."

What kind of response do you think you would get to an answer like that? It's simple. They would think you're crazy! Justifiably so - because to expect that you would end up at the right destination with such a general, unclear idea of where you're headed would be ridiculous.

Yet it's amazing how many people take that exact approach when it comes to their lives. They don't plan. They don't give conscious thought to exactly what they want and what's at stake around making those outcomes a reality in their lives. They don't set clear, specific, measurable goals with definite timelines.

This reminds me of a study conducted at the Harvard Business School MBA program back in 1979. Now, that's close to 40 years ago from the time of this book. But the lesson here is so profound, that it's worth reviewing.

In the book *What They Don't Teach You at Harvard Business School*, Mark McCormack tells of a study conducted on students in the 1979 Harvard MBA program. In that year, the students were asked, "Have you set clear, written goals for your future and made plans to accomplish them?" Only 3% of the graduates had written goals and plans; 13% had goals, but they were not in writing; and a whopping 84% had no specific goals at all.

Ten years later, the members of the class were interviewed again, and the findings, while perhaps predictable, were nonetheless astonishing. **The 13% of the class who had goals were earning, on average,**

twice as much as the 84% who had no goals at all! And what about the 3% who had clear, written goals? They were earning, on average, **ten times as much as the other 97% combined!**

I would like you to consider those numbers for a moment. Ten times as much!

And this doesn't mention the other parts of the study, which may have been a bit more intangible, but still striking. The top 3% who had clear, written goals were also happier, better adjusted and more confident in their abilities as human beings. But I guess that's a bit easier to achieve when you're earning ten times as much as the people you are being compared to.

THE STORY OF HAILE GEBRSELASSIE

It's one thing to quote studies. But I'd like to share a real life story that illustrates the sheer power of being crystal clear on your outcomes. That is the story of Haile Gebrselassie.

This is an individual who, when you consider his life story and the circumstances he started from, and what he accomplished in the face of these, it isn't just extraordinary. It's mind blowing. And it should truly put into perspective and I'll even say eliminate any doubt you might have around any of the challenges or barriers you may be dealing with.

Haile Gebrselassie was born in a rural area of Ethiopia, called Asella. He was born one of ten brothers and sisters. Now unlike in the United States for example, in Africa when you say rural, what you're actually saying is poor. His father was a peasant farmer, and would beat Haile and all of his children on a regular basis.

The entire family lived in a one-room hut called a tukul, made of thatched wood and straw, with a mud floor. As soon as he walked out of his door, Haile was surrounded by farm animals and the smells and droppings that come along with that.

Haile would begin every day with his morning chores and then he was immediately off to school. And these weren't regular chores; these were farm chores. We're not talking about making your bed or throwing out the garbage.

But what was interesting about his trip to school is he had to run six miles each way back and forth every day, barefoot, on hard clay roads and hard, prickly grass and straw, holding his books and writing utensils while he ran.

There was no getting a lift from his parents, no buses.

Because of his morning chores and the fact that his father had no leniency with this, despite running full speed the entire way, he would often show up to school late. Now in Ethiopia, at least at the time, their way of dealing with lateness was a bit different than ours here in the states. It wasn't a mark on your record. He would get whipped or lashed in front of his entire class as soon as he got there.

Once school was over, he would head right back home, running full steam the entire way back as well. As soon as he got home, no after school snack, no Internet. He'd pop right back into the field with his father and siblings, and get right back to work. Where his father would immediately yell at him and beat him for being late and lazy again, even though he just got back from school! He got it coming and going.

And if he ever wanted to take even a little time off of the farm for some fun and leisure, what do you think would happen when he returned? Exactly, he'd be yelled at and beaten. Told he was no good, lazy, that his priorities were off and he didn't appreciate anything.

And oh yes, in addition to that, every day he would have to go with his mother or other siblings to collect water for the family at a not-so-nearby water hole, which would take another three hours. Quite a lifestyle for a young boy, yes?

In addition, his family and his entire village lived under the constant threat of violence. Tribal conflicts, struggles for political power, gunrunners and the like created an environment of constant threat and fear. Attacks, killings, cease fires, new conflicts. I'm sure you've heard of some of the atrocities that have occurred in different parts of Africa. I think you'd agree, that right there is more than enough to have to deal with when you start out in life. Yes?

But one of the things his entire family had in addition to each other was a deep belief in God and an incredible work ethic. Something else Haile in particular had going for him, to escape and let go of the pressure he was constantly under, was running. He'd just run and run and run for long distances and push his body to the point of exhaustion.

But then something else happened. He lost his mother, with whom he was very close, to sickness when he was just seven years old. Losing your Mother as a fully-grown man or woman is traumatic enough. Imagine having that happen to you when you were only seven, with nine other siblings and a father who beat you regularly. But one thing remained constant throughout that. He stayed clear and he continued to run.

Now let me ask you, how do you think his father felt about his running? Do you think he saw it as a wise, practical thing that would help the family and put food on the table? Of course not! He would yell at his son and chastise him for it. "Why do you run? What use is this? How is this going to help the family? I want you to stop this, now!"

Haile was a very obedient son. But this was one thing he would not give up. He couldn't. It was one of the few things that kept him connected to himself. One of the few things that kept him sane.

So he continued to run, and somewhere around this time he developed the dream of someday representing his country and running for Ethiopia in the Olympic games. It was just a fantasy. But it gave him strength and a sense of hope and purpose, and helped him to get through the difficulties.

He didn't know how and if you think about it on paper, it's a crazy idea. He was the son of a peasant farmer, living in the middle of nowhere in one of the poorest countries in the world. But he maintained his dream, he was clear and he continued to run. And it's interesting: very often the universe has a way of taking care of you when you're clear and you show it that you want something badly enough.

When he was a bit older, one day he was out running, as he would often do for hours at a time around the outskirts of his village. He happened upon a group of other runners, who happened to be a running club. They would run and work on their technique together and push one another to higher levels. They had an experienced instructor who was mentoring them. Upon seeing Haile's commitment to his running, the instructor invited him to join their club. This was to be, no doubt, a life altering experience for Haile.

Under the tutelage of his teacher and with the support of his club, he took his technique, stamina and endurance to new levels. His ability continued to improve until he finally decided to move to the city of Addis Ababa, where he moved in with his brother, to be able to focus exclusively on his running and join an even bigger running club.

In Addis Ababa, there is horrendous poverty. It seems there are more homeless than those who have a roof over their head. There are people sleeping on the streets everywhere; squatters and shantytowns everywhere you look. It looks like the Great Depression times ten. It's difficult to even look at—and this is a major city we're talking about.

Now, you might think you know where this is going—he made this big move to the city, he sacrificed and then everything came together and he was a big champion. Right? Far from it.

In his first major race, after having already practiced and pushed himself to what he thought were his limits his entire life, he finished 99th. 99th! His body collapsed dehydrated, in massive cramps right after he passed the finish line. His brother had to carry him home. And this was just a local race. Not too encouraging. But what remained constant is—he was clear, he maintained his dream and he continued to run.

What happened after that? Another two years of constant, hard, dedicated training and sacrifice. He found reservoirs of speed and stamina within himself that he didn't know existed. He was *committed*.

Remember that thing about the universe I just mentioned? Well it turns out that the man who was the head of his running club, whom he just happened upon, eventually introduced Haile to the woman who was to be his future wife.

She was a lovely woman named Alem, who went on to support him and believe in his dream right along with him, unconditionally. Even when members of his own family did not.

He continued to improve until finally, it happened. *He was chosen to represent Ethiopia in the 1996 Olympics in Atlanta.* Can you believe it? Ethiopia may not be that strong in most Olympic Sports, but the one sport they do excel in and have a long tradition of excellence in is running. The competition nationwide is fierce, and Haile was chosen. Rather astounding.

I think that alone would be a major success story and we could stop right there. He would always have a job as a running coach or instructor. While it might not have made him a wealthy man, in a country where there is so much poverty, he would never have to worry about being able to support himself and his family again.

Another fact about long distance running in Ethiopia is that for many decades, they've had an intense rivalry with Kenya. Kenya too has a very long tradition of greatness in that sport and has won many medals. Haile was going to be running against the man who was considered to be the greatest long distance runner in the world at the time, and favored to win the 10,000 meter race— considered to be the ultimate test of human endurance—a Kenyan named Paul Tergat. This was Haile's nemesis.

I wonder what it feels like to know that you're representing the hopes and dreams of an entire nation, based on how you perform in one race. For the first time in his life, Haile flew on a big plane to another part of the world—and to compete at the highest level.

The contest was close and tightly contested for most of the race. Then towards the end, with only four laps left to go, Tergat from Kenya attempted to pull away from the pack. There was only one other runner who stayed with him. You can guess who it was: Haile. Two lone warriors running for greatness, honor and their countries in front of an audience of billions. They stayed neck and neck.

During that time when he was pushing his body beyond its limits, all of the hardship—running twelve miles to and from school every day, working for hours on the farm in the scorching sun, beatings from his father, the loss of his mother—all came to Haile like spirit visions, while he continued to pray to God.

Then, when the bell rang for the last lap, something extraordinary happened. Haile found something deep within himself. He kicked into another gear and began to pull away from the Kenyan. And the lead grew longer—and longer. The crowd surged, his countrymen and women wherever they were sprang up and screamed, his family back home jumped and screamed; his father watching on television from the other side of the world the entire time.

And then it happened. Haile Gebrselassie, this quiet, soft-spoken man, son of a peasant farmer in one of the poorest countries in the world, won the 1996 Olympic 10,000 meter race by a blowout. He was the champion, the best in the world. He had done it. He had brought glory to his family, his village and his entire nation.

When he returned home, he received a hero's greeting from over a million people! Have you ever seen a crowd of over one million people? I haven't.

Runner's World Magazine, the premiere runner's magazine in the U.S., proclaimed him to be the greatest long distance runner of all time. He is now a national hero and a living legend in his country.

Amazing, yes? The power of being clear and staying true to your commitments. But this was real. *All due to the power of clarity.*

THE POWER OF BEING CLEAR ON YOUR WHY

So being crystal clear on what you want to achieve is no doubt critical.

Setting clear, specific, measurable goals with definite timelines is a vital aspect of that process.

But I've got some news for you. If setting goals is all you're doing, it's not enough! I know I just mentioned how great goals are and how important they are. But if you're simply setting goals and that's all, it's a good start and you're putting yourself into the top 3% of the population by doing that, but it's still not enough.

Now why is that? Because as important as getting clear is—and make no mistake, it is vital—there is another key component that must come right along with it. If not, your approach will be incomplete and you still run the risk of being derailed and uprooted when it really matters.

And that is you must also get clear on your *why. Why* you want your desired outcome. What's at stake for you? What will having that outcome *give* you? Why is not having that outcome absolutely unacceptable?

Now, why is being clear on your "why" critical as well? Why is this so important? Why is just getting clear on your outcomes not enough?

That's because like it or not, most of the time when you're up to big things in your life, setbacks, upset and adversity will usually show up. That's just a fact of life. I don't claim to fully understand exactly why this happens. Maybe it's the universe's way of testing you, to see how badly you really want what you claim to. But at some point, this just seems to come with the territory.

Well, when those challenges come, you need to be crystal clear on *why* you're doing what you're doing in the first place. Why is it a must, not just a should? Why will you be willing to put up with whatever you have to, endure the unendurable, do whatever it takes to stay the course and follow through?

I call this getting leverage on yourself. This is the power of tapping into your driving force. What's really *behind* the goals you set and the outcomes you commit to in your life?

You want to look at your *why* from two separate perspectives. Yes, you definitely want to get clear on what having a goal will give you and why it will be great to accomplish it and all of the inspiring, motivating reasons for making it a reality, but I also encourage you to look at the flip side as well. What is the price you will pay if you *don't* achieve it? Why is *not* having that goal absolutely unacceptable? Why will you do everything within your power to avoid having to be without it?

You want to motivate your brain on both sides of the coin, so that achieving that goal is a given. It's a foregone conclusion, it's done, it's a slam- dunk! And you'll find that being clear on your goals and the whys behind them will be a strong driver behind your activity and the production you achieve.

If you recall the pain/pleasure principle, very often human beings will do just as much if not more to avoid failure, than they will to achieve success. I'm not saying it makes sense and I'm certainly not looking to analyze why and figure it all out. I'm simply observing the facts. Many people are driven by the fear of failure. So why not use both of these powerful drives, the carrot and the stick, to move you forward and create the outcome you desire? Make sense?

Most people set New Year's resolutions. They set a bunch of goals and they get all excited about how this year is going to be the year that they *really do it*. Then they completely forget about their goals for the next six months or so.

Then they happen to come across them somewhere or they're somehow reminded of them again, and it's sort of like, "Oh yeah! I remember that." And they repeat this same pattern year after year.

Do you know anyone like that? Might they be closer than you care to admit? Might that person be you?

Of course not, but just in case remember, if you want to get results you've never gotten before, sometimes you must be willing to do things you've never before done. You must be willing to stretch your comfort zone and step outside of the box.

Next, most people never set goals or take the time to really get clear on their desired outcomes, because they take the process of goal setting entirely for granted. We've all heard about the idea of setting goals so many times before that the importance of goal setting tends to get diluted.

Don't get caught up in the law of familiarity. Setting goals and getting clear is crucial! That will never change. Sometimes in life you simply have to honor the fundamentals.

Furthermore, most people simply don't realize the true power of setting goals. They view it merely as an academic exercise; this list that they have to write down, as if they were going to the grocery store or something.

Understand that with goals, you are creating your future in advance. When you lay out your goals clearly and powerfully, you are literally crafting a destiny and shaping your life. Goals can create the power to make us grow and expand as human beings. This is not to be taken lightly. Have fun with it for sure, but please do not take it lightly.

I can tell you some brief examples in my own life. Growing up first in Queens and then Brooklyn, New York, one of my dreams was always to live in a beautiful apartment in a beautiful building in a nice neighborhood in Manhattan. Many kids who grow up in the boroughs, as they're called, or the suburbs of New York at one point or another, have that as a goal. And as you may have heard before, regardless of where you live, it's not exactly cheap to live in Manhattan.

But it can be a pretty awesome experience.

Well, I've lived in NYC now for over fifteen years, and when I moved in, there weren't any roommates. That place was mine. And yes, I'm in a beautiful doorman building in one of the nicest neighborhoods in the city. I have the United Nations, the Chrysler Building, Grand Central Station, The Ford Foundation, Times Square, even Central Park, all within walking distance of my building. It's been amazing. And it's to the point where now, quite frankly, I don't even think twice about it. All those places you see in *Sex and the City* are my neighborhood.

I also used to dream about doing the kind of work where I can make a nice living, while impacting people on a massive scale and really making a difference. Where I could be a public speaker and really move people with the words I say and the ideas that I share. Well, I've been a professional coach, author and speaker now for over fifteen years. I've made so many friends and touched so many lives; it's been amazing. Sometimes I have to pinch myself to confirm that it's real.

I also used to dream that I would be able to create a lifestyle for myself where I could come and go as I pleased and I'd be able to travel to new and interesting places. I mean, isn't that part of the fun of life—travel and discovery?

Well, as I write these words, in the last ninety days alone I've traveled to Fort Lauderdale, Miami, Key Largo, Los Angeles, Venice Beach, Waikiki, the Bahamas and Hong Kong. And the Hong Kong trip was paid for, because it was for business. The next trip I'm planning is to a beautiful island in the Philippines. Why? Because I can!

I don't say that arrogantly and I'm not saying that every ninety-day period of my life looks exactly like that. I say that because I'm stoked, and *so* thankful to be able to do that!

Two years ago I set a goal that I would lose thirty pounds and keep it off. Well, I lost forty pounds in under four months and I've kept most of it off. How do you not feel powerful and excited about life when you keep achieving the goals that you set for yourself? I'm sharing this because hopefully some examples from my own life can serve as an illustration and even an inspiration for what you can create for yourself.

Now would you like to know the one common denominator all of these goals I've achieved and many more have in common? First, at some point I got clear and I wrote them down. I made them tangible. I had something to look at and review. And I got crystal clear with myself on exactly *why* I wanted to achieve those goals. Why they were an absolute must and why I was willing to do whatever it took to make them a reality. In other words, I got clear! I know I'm saying this word "clear" and emphasizing it a lot. But that's because I really want you to get it, and I know this alone can make such a critical difference in your life when you really take it in and apply it.

Then, I mentioned those goals to other people in my life who I knew would check in on me and hold me accountable. Even the very book you're reading right now was one of those goals. It took longer than planned to finally bring this to market and there were people in my life who would follow up and ask me— sometimes supportively and sometimes judgmentally, "When is your book coming out?" That was one of the driving forces that ensured I would complete this project. And it happened.

Don't you see, there's a formula here. It works, but you've got to work it. When you set goals, something happens. You become a creator, a manifestor.

Let's take the story of Gandhi. You know—the father of modern day India. How realistic do you think it would have initially sounded if someone said that this one man would be able to single-handedly begin an international movement that ultimately drove the British, the greatest colonial power throughout history, out of India, simply through nonviolent protest? Quite frankly, it would have been laughable. But he did.

If someone had traveled back in time to the 1940s and attempted to explain the concept of the Internet, or Facebook or email, what kind of response do you think that would have received?

Who the hell knows what realistic is? Don't worry about that. Be willing to dream big. Get clear on your goal, get clear on why, write it down, review it often, share it with others, and then get busy.

And don't worry about knowing exactly how you're going to accomplish everything. Remember—reasons come first, answers come second. "Why to" first. "How to" second." When you're willing to commit to a goal and get into action, you'd be amazed how often the answers and breakthroughs will reveal themselves.

The magic that you've heard about setting goals and getting clear is real. Thoughts really are things. What we focus on consistently does tend to show up in our lives. I'm not saying it's a magic formula and that you don't have to work, sometimes incredibly hard, that you don't have to sacrifice and deal with life's delays for it to show up. But very often it will.

When you set a goal, you are acknowledging to your conscious and subconscious minds that where you're at is not good enough. And understand that dissatisfaction is not something to hide out or run away from. It is a truly awesome power to harness. Some of the greatest accomplishments and success stories throughout history have come from a deep sense of incompleteness or dissatisfaction.

But you must be willing to access it. Gandhi was not satisfied. Bill Gates was not satisfied. Haile Gebreselassie was not satisfied. I can tell you from my own experience, I love what I do and I'm very happy to be doing it. And I'm not satisfied.

And realize, that just as important as what getting clear and achieving goals will give you, is who they will make of you as a person. At the end of your life, all you're really going to have is what you've accomplished, who you've become and the lives that you've touched. You can't take the *things* with you. So remember to set inspiring, meaningful goals. This is your life we're talking about.

So get excited and get ready. It's time to take your life to the next level and beyond! When you're done reading this chapter, I encourage you to put aside some time, even just ten to fifteen minutes, and write down both your top personal and professional goals. Then write down why they are a must and what's at stake around them.

On that topic, if you'd like to step into that in some more detail, I have an entire track on goal setting in the *Samurai of Sales* audio program, called "Outcome Clarification: The Power of Effective Goal Setting." In that recording, I walk you through a comprehensive "real time" goal setting workshop that will get you crystal clear on your top personal and professional goals for the next twelve months of your life. And perhaps even more importantly, I will assist you in getting clear on why those outcomes are an absolute *must*. If you want to check that out, go to:

www.samuraiofsales.com/product/the-samurai-of-sales-audiobook/

REVIEW:

- Regardless of how much you may have going for you, if you are not crystal clear on your desired outcome, you will always struggle in hitting your mark—especially in the world of professional sales.
- Being clear gives your mind a direction to move in.
- If you want to make it to the top of the mountain of professional sales, you're going to have to deal with a lot of nonsense and take a lot of crap to get there.
- If you are not crystal clear on why you're dealing with all of that, you run a much greater risk of being derailed and taken off track.

- A study conducted with the graduating MBA class at Harvard in 1979 showed that the 3% of students who were crystal clear on their desired outcomes and had them written down, were on average earning ten times as much as the other 97% combined ten years later.
- Haile Gebrselassie, the Ethiopian long distance runner who won the 10,000 meter Olympic race in 1996 after overcoming tremendous adversity in his life, is a truly inspirational example of what someone can achieve when they are crystal clear on their outcome.
- You want to motivate your mind on both the pain and pleasure sides of the coin—why something is important to you as well as what you stand to lose if you do not make that outcome a reality.
- Most people take getting clear and setting goals for granted. They don't give it the attention and energy it truly deserves.
- I have many examples in my own life, and I know many other people who have achieved tremendous outcomes in their lives as a result of getting clear, setting goals, writing them down and reviewing them often.

9

SAMURAI TOOLBOX

ADDITIONAL TIPS

In this chapter, I have included a general collection of tips and insights that can help you thrive in any market or economy. Each of these ideas could take up an entire chapter unto themselves, and I feel that any book on sales mastery would be incomplete without them. Have fun, and I encourage you to apply these in a way that works for you and your style.

GETTING HELP FROM OUTSIDE SOURCES OR PEOPLE

Very simply put, be willing to get help. Often, this is much easier said than done. At one time or another, we all need help. We don't have it all figured out.

You might want to say the following statements out loud and repeat them numerous times:

"There are times when I need help!"
"I don't have it all figured out!"

Imagine looking someone else in the eye while you are saying this one:

"There is something you know here that I don't, and I could use your help!"

Do you realize how intensely difficult it is for most people just to make these three statements? Be honest, when you were saying those things out loud (if indeed you were), didn't it feel a little unnatural, as if you were a little out of your element? Mark McCormick, the billionaire founder of International Management Group (IMG) and the gentleman who basically invented the sports agency industry, once said during an interview: *"One of the keys to success in business is to surround yourself with people who are smarter than you are."* Mr. McCormick knows a thing or two about success.

THE MASTERMIND

In addition to accessing information and resources you would not have had otherwise, there is another reason to get support from other people: you get to tap into one of the most powerful principles known to the human condition, at least in regards to stimulating the mind and manifesting superior results, and that is what is commonly referred to as the **"mastermind."**

What an important, vital and incredibly powerful tool to utilize.

This term was first coined by the great Napoleon Hill in the 1930s in his book *Think and Grow Rich*, and it has forever changed the way success-oriented people think and go about creating true abundance and prosperity in their lives.

Simply put, the mastermind is defined as "coordination of knowledge and effort, in a spirit of harmony between two or more people, for the attainment of a definite purpose." The core philosophy behind the concept of the mastermind is that the collective intelligence created when two or more minds come together on a particular topic or project is *far superior* to the intelligence of each mind individually. As Mr. Hill goes on to say, "No two minds ever come together without, thereby, creating a third, invisible, intangible force which may be likened to a third mind."

This often seems to have a magical, mythical power that you cannot point to externally but is undeniable in its impact and in the energy you get from being around it.

SURROUND YOURSELF WITH PEOPLE WHO TRULY WANT TO SEE YOU SUCCEED

Another reason getting help from outside sources and people is so critical is because it puts you in touch with another key aspect of attaining success and accomplishing the results you are truly committed to, and that is *surrounding yourself with people who truly want to see you succeed.*

Very often, that is *much* easier said than done. Why? First of all, like it or not, the reality is that there are a lot of people out there who—for whatever reason—do not want to see you succeed. It could be jealousy or competition or the fact that they attempted certain things in their own life and it didn't work out for them. Or it could be that they would never even dream of attempting what you're up to, and the thought of you actually accomplishing it scares the hell out of them. Whatever the particular reason may be, the simple fact of life is that these people, often referred to as "dream stealers," are all around you—and they are not always easy to detect.

Are you ready for some more lovely news? A lot of these people are already planted within *your own camp*: they are within your own circle of friends, associates, acquaintances, and, dare I say it, possibly *even within your own family!*

Yes, there may very well be people within your own family—extended or direct—who really do genuinely love you but who wouldn't be all that jazzed about the prospect of you experiencing massive success and fulfillment—at least, not beyond a level they have deemed appropriate for you. They may act like they want success for you, or even truly *believe* they do. They may say nice things and seem totally supportive, at least on the surface. But when push comes to shove and you *really* start making some forward progress, or when something you're doing conflicts with one of their agendas, their true intentions or feelings will come out.

Have you ever had this experience with someone, even to a small degree? Most of us have at one time or another. Have you ever *been* that person—the one doling out the negativity towards another's success, and didn't even realize it until later on (perhaps a huge "aha" moment for you here)? Once again, there could be a slew of different and complex reasons for this to occur, and I am not going to delve too deeply into that conversation here. But the fact is, this is a part of life and a part of your journey towards success in any endeavor— especially professional sales.

I am going to tell you why it can be so difficult to surround yourself with people who genuinely want to see you succeed. I'm going to be a bit blunt here; I'm not going to sugarcoat this. Once again, this is a study in how life really is— not how we want it to be. Fair enough?

The reason it is difficult is because *very often surrounding yourself primarily or exclusively with people who truly want to see you succeed can mean first having to separate and distance yourself from those who truly* don't *want to see you succeed.* Creating the space for the right people to show up means first getting the "wrong" people out of the way.

This can be more challenging than you might think, because it can involve distancing yourself and, in some cases, completely disconnecting from people who have already been in your life for *years*—some of whom you have known since you were a child or for your *entire life!*

Think about that. Isn't that a bit counterintuitive? Maybe so, but it is also *critical*, especially when you're looking to create a new self-concept, set of patterns, or possibilities for yourself around *anything*. I'm not saying that you have to totally shun or disregard someone, or start acting negatively towards them (especially in the case of family, because let's face it: family is family).

But would you agree that ultimately it is *you* who is responsible for who you hang out with, whom you spend most of your time with, and whom you let into your own mind? And if there is someone in your inner circle it doesn't serve you to spend time with, might it be in your best interests to begin to distance yourself?

I can tell you that in my life, there are literally *childhood friends* whom I still have love for and would be there for at a moment's notice, but from whom I have distanced myself. In some cases, I don't hang out with them at all, because somewhere along the line it became crystal clear to me that it just did not serve me to be around them a whole lot; on some level, they were stifling my growth or development, or they were not as supportive of my success as I used to think they were. That's the reality.

There was no big blowout or bad blood or anything like that in any of these cases, and I am certainly not saying that they're bad people or that I'm better than them or *anything* to that effect. I'm just saying it was time to move on. They are now in the wake (the water wake, not the funeral wake) of my life instead of right in front of me.

Often times, people like that don't consciously realize what they're doing or how it is affecting you. In those rare cases where someone is consciously or maliciously trying to sabotage your success, then of course you *definitely* want to distance yourself as much as possible and as quickly as possible; but in most cases, it is not that black and white. If I got that call at three in the morning telling me they needed me, I would be there in a heartbeat. It's simply that I decided it wasn't in my best interests to spend the majority of my time around them.

If you're wrestling with this one or if it feels a little strange to contemplate, which I understand, just let it sit for a little while and give it an opportunity to sink in. You may find that you'll get a little more clarity with this when you give your mind an opportunity to work with it and stop judging what you feel about this.

Ultimately, if this doesn't work for you, hey, it's your life; you're welcome to take from this advice what works for you and leave the rest. Okay?

I understand I'm handing you a true dose of reality here. I may be forcing you to take a look at some circumstances or relationships in your life that you have not consciously considered before. Reading this chapter may ultimately lead you to make some difficult and life-changing decisions.

If so, *great!* For one simple reason: *this is your life!* Time is precious and the longer you accept circumstances or relationships that do not serve you or that are not moving you forward, the longer you deprive yourself of attaining those things or reaching the heights you are truly capable of. And remember, what you are capable of is limitless!

BE WILLING TO ANSWER A QUESTION WITH A QUESTION

When we are children, we're conditioned to believe that answering a question with another question is somehow rude or disrespectful—that you're not being truly straight with someone when you do that. That was perhaps valid in some instances when we were growing up, because we were usually speaking to our parents, teachers, coaches, religious leaders or someone else who was there to guide and mentor us. In those situations, responding back with a question may have thwarted the learning process or simply been a sign of disrespect. Yet once again, this vital question comes up:

Do the habits and ways of thinking that may have served and protected us as children necessarily give us the results that we are looking for as adults?

You know the answer to this: not necessarily and usually not!

When in a sales dialogue of any kind, the best way to respond to a question is usually with another question. You are getting your point across by letting the prospect tell himself, while simultaneously maintaining control of the conversation. Remember, people love to give their own opinions on a topic, even (and especially) after they have just asked someone else a question. Have you ever noticed, sometimes people will ask you a question just so they can have a chance to express their own opinion on that topic?

In some instances, giving a flat-out answer first may be the right move, because your prospect may need some substantive information or just want to feel like you are being straight. And that can often be a buying signal. But even in those cases, after you have given a straight answer, you want to go right back to being the one asking the questions. For example:

> **Prospect:** What has your company's retention of existing clients been over the last five years?
>
> **You:** A little over 90%. Is that something that you consider to be a key consideration in your decision?

Some good transition, segue-type phrases you can say to begin answering a question with a question are:

"Well, [*pause*] let me ask you ..."

"That's a good question, and that brings up a very important point."

"To help me answer that as best I can, can I ask you a question?"

"I'll actually get to that in a moment. Before I do, let me ask you a question ..."

"And on that topic ..."

For example:

Prospect: "How much does it cost?"

You: That is always the question, isn't it? There are a few answers to that, depending on how we proceed. So that I can give you the most accurate answer on that, let me ask you a few questions ...

Or:

Prospect: Why is your price_____% higher than ABC competitor?

You: Well [*prospect's name*], there are a few reasons for that. But first let me ask you, in your experience, do superior products and services usually cost more or less?

Or:

Prospect: What's the best offer you can make me?

You: So I know that we're at least in the same ballpark, what did you have in mind?

As long as you are asking your question(s) to make or bring up a valid point and do it in the tone and rhythm of the conversation you are already having, you will be amazed at how smoothly this lands and how receptive your prospects are to having their questions answered with questions.

KEEP YOUR MIND CENTERED

Amidst all the quantitative *"hard"* skills and techniques I teach entrepreneurs on how to generate better results and be more successful, there is one less obvious, less tangible skill that is a common thread through everything, and it is perhaps the most important of all: **keeping your mind centered.**

It's simple. When your mind is sharp, focused and centered, you can hone in and operate at your best. When it is not, you could be armed with the best selling tools on the planet and it won't mean a thing. When you are in a sales dialogue, whether at the very first contact or at the closing table, you need to know exactly where you are in the conversation and where you are going.

One misstep, one hiccup, can totally disrupt your momentum and change the tone and direction of the conversation. We've all had that experience: that sinking feeling of having a conversation or rapport slowly slipping away from us. Being sharp, connected and "dialed in" can be the critical difference that separates staying on track from losing the connection.

One of the things that distinguishes the skill of keeping your mind centered from many other critical selling skills is it usually depends much more on what you have done *prior to* your conversation with your prospect, rather than what you are actually doing in that moment.

That brings me to three vital questions to consider when you are entering into any kind of presentation or selling situation:

1. Are You Prepared?

Do you know what you need to about your product/service? Do you know what you need to about your prospect? Do you already know exactly where you intend to take the conversation and how you plan on getting there? Are you prepared for the unexpected? Are you ready to focus on the questions you can ask, instead of on the statements you will make? Have you already considered the predominant objections you will probably hear, and have you practiced, rehearsed and role-played how you will handle them *when* (not *if*) they come up?

2. Are You Mentally Fit?

Is your mind clear? Did you do your best to get adequate rest the night before? Did you eat a large meal before going to sleep? Are you hung over? Have you cleared your mind of distractions before getting on the phone or going into that appointment? Can you make an agreement with yourself that you'll revisit any unresolved issues or conflicts after your sales call?

Do you attempt to multitask while making sales calls? If yes, I have a question: if someone called you (legitimately) to let you know you had just won $10,000,000 in the lottery, and they wanted to confirm you did in fact have the winning numbers, would you multitask during that conversation or give it your full, undivided attention? In other words, if the task at hand is important enough, you will give it the attention it deserves. There are times when multitasking is a good idea, but during sales calls is not one of them.

Do you engage in any ongoing disciplines to consistently strengthen your mind? Things like meditation, yoga and observing your breathing are no longer considered strange practices from the Far East; they have been proven scientifically to work in a very big way. I can tell you that they have made a very big difference in my own life. And of course, there is always the power of prayer.

3. Do You Believe?

Are you confident in your product or service? Do you truly believe it can serve your prospect and provide her with the solution she is looking for? Do you truly believe it is worth the extra money when compared with your competition? As I'm sure you already know, your prospect will always find *someone* who is cheaper than you are, whether it's real or imagined.

Are you confident in yourself? Do you truly believe you do a good job for your clients and that any prospect would be incredibly lucky to have the opportunity to work with you? Do you know yourself to be someone who operates with integrity? Do you go the extra mile for your clients? Can you be trusted?

Yes, I have laid out a healthy short list for you here. They all intermingle and feed off of each other in one way or another, and they are all critically important. Understanding that, I have two more important questions for you to consider:

1. **If you cannot answer "yes" to all three of the above questions, how can you expect to keep your mind centered and clear on a consistent basis?**
2. **If you don't consistently keep your mind centered, how can you ever expect to operate at your best or experience your true potential?**

Do whatever it takes. Commit to keeping your mind centered and focused. When you do, you'll find *everything* you are doing much easier—and your results will skyrocket! If you have been thinking about taking some specific steps in regards to strengthening and conditioning your mind, and you're not quite sure how or where to look, please feel free to give my office a call. We'd love to help you with that.

HAVE FUN WITH YOUR MISTAKES

Did you know that making mistakes, screwing up and dropping the ball are just as inevitable as are doing things right and executing flawlessly? Like it or not, that's a fact. I am not saying you should strive for subpar performance or accept patterns where you continually make the same, mindless mistakes. What I am saying is, if you know mistakes are going to occur from time to time and you know they are an inevitable part of the human condition, why not laugh and have fun with them when they show up? Treat them as valuable learning experiences instead of attacking yourself and constantly making yourself wrong.

Making mistakes somewhere along the line is as inevitable as breathing. I'm curious, every time that you take a breath, do you say things to yourself like, "Damn! What the hell is my problem? Why am I such an idiot? Why can't I ever get things right? Alright, I'm never doing that again! Oh, I just give up!"

I certainly hope not.

GO TO THE SEMINARS. WORK ON YOURSELF

Imagine if you wanted to be a surgeon, but you were of the opinion that medical school wasn't for you. Or you wanted to be an attorney, but you were clear that law school was out of the question. I'm sure you'd agree there would be a major disconnect there.

Well, in essence, that is the same philosophy you are operating from if you claim you want to be a master sales professional but are not willing to engage in ongoing training and cultivation of your selling skills. Luckily (or perhaps not), in the world of professional sales, we are not required to gain a degree from a nationally accredited selling school to be allowed to sell. This, of course, is not referring to any professional licenses you may have to acquire for your particular industry, nor does it refer to the standard training program your company may offer for new reps—which I'm sure is just fine.

I mean a school with a two- or three-year program specifically focused on your education and mastery of all the skills you need to succeed as a sales professional. If there were, I'd be curious to see how salesmanship and closing ability worldwide would elevate. In my opinion, that would be pretty neat.

But since we don't have anything like that, what you have is the majority of entrepreneurs and sales professionals worldwide who believe that attending training events or engaging in ongoing education is unnecessary and in some cases just hokey. I will grant that over the last fifteen to twenty years—thanks in part to individuals like Tony Robbins, Brian Tracy, Zig Ziglar, Tom Hopkins and the like—ongoing training and professional development have become more mainstream and accepted.

But as someone who has been out in the field promoting to corporations all over the United States for over fifteen years, I still consistently see that—as an overwhelming rule—the majority of people would rather *not* make the investment and go through the inconvenience of registering for programs that would offer them the exact tools and skills they need to be great. What's even more astounding is that when the organization pays for them to go, very often attendance rates drop off even more! Or when people come, they end up leaving early.

My advice is simple: if you want to get a black belt in karate, go to the dojo, learn, take instruction and practice consistently—and eventually you will get your belt. If you want to be a master swordsman, learn, take instruction, practice consistently—and eventually you will master the sword. The samurai considered his sword to be an extension of his soul. If you want to be a sales samurai, *go to the seminars,* learn, take instruction, get coaching, practice consistently... and eventually you will be a master.

ALWAYS LOOK FOR WHAT'S BEYOND THE WORDS

In any conversation, there are usually two levels of communication:

1. The words that are being said.
2. What is beyond, behind or beneath the words.

For example, someone might say the words, "I just want something that is reasonably priced," but what they are really thinking is, "Show me something that excites me and gives me more prestige."

You can usually pick up on what is behind someone's words by paying attention to things like body language, voice cues, the volume and pace at which they are speaking, words they tend to emphasize, questions they don't answer completely, etc... Very often it is what's *not* said that reveals the most. It is in paying attention to these cues that you can get a true read on where your prospect is at and what it will really take to hit his hot button.

This is often referred to as "the elusive obvious." It's right in front of us, but we're too busy either waiting to speak or focusing on the words being said, not considering what is underneath or beyond them.

Also remember that, as human beings, we make decisions for emotional reasons and attempt to justify those decisions with logic. In other words, often times there is what we are *telling* ourselves we feel or want, and then there is how we really feel. Sometimes we can't even tell the difference until it is time to act! How often have you had the experience in which you told yourself you were going to think, act or feel a certain way around something, but when push came to shove, you acted in a completely different manner—as if a completely different person had emerged?

This is human nature.

Find the language behind the language.

ESTABLISHING CREDIBILITY IS CRUCIAL

Something you must realize about *everything* I have covered throughout this entire book is that it will mean nothing at all if you do not have *credibility* with your prospect. He must believe that you know what you are talking about or that you have direct access to someone who does. He must also believe that you have his best interests in mind. Otherwise, anything you say will go in one ear and out of the other. Some great ways to establish credibility are to:

1. Be completely truthful in the things you say and the claims you make. Don't lie.

2. Represent a company that has a great reputation in your industry.

3. If you represent a lesser-known company, be equipped with a strong, persuasive rationale as to why you choose to work with a smaller, more customized boutique firm.

4. Provide referrals or references that carry a lot of credibility.

5. Display a high level of understanding of the prospect's business or the industry she is in.

6. Show a strong knowledge and understanding of your competition, and show it in a way that, of course, ultimately makes you the better choice.

7. Be the "expert" in your industry or display direct access to someone who is.

CREATE URGENCY: THE MISSING LINK

This is very often the one critical element missing from an otherwise flawless presentation or closing conversation. Your prospect may like you and your product/service, he may be amenable to the terms you are proposing and even have a need for your solution, but if he does not perceive the need to take action now, he usually won't.

It is your job to create that urgency. You can do this by offering a limited time on your terms or on the availability of your product/service. You can do this by emphasizing the pain or loss your prospect is experiencing and will continue to experience by not taking action today. Or you can get your prospect excited about how great it will be once he has made the decision to come on board.

However you do it, the bottom line is that you *must* create that sense of urgency, and—of course—any term you impose upon your prospect to create this urgency must be real. If you continue to impose terms that are not real, you will lose credibility and eventually the entire relationship.

BE WILLING TO HEAR YOUR PROSPECT'S HONEST OPINION

Very often salespeople will orchestrate their presentations in a way that avoids or sidesteps having to hear the prospect say anything negative or disagreeable. The thinking behind this is that if the prospect isn't saying anything disagreeable, then he must not be thinking anything disagreeable; or, why make the conversation any more difficult than it needs to be?

Nothing could be farther from the truth!

Directing the topic of conversation does not necessarily mean you are directing what your prospect is thinking or feeling. You must find out any issues or concerns she harbors in regards to you, your organization, your industry or your offering. I would go so far as to say that you want to *seek out* your prospect's concerns, even if it makes the conversation more challenging temporarily, because if you don't find them, you can't deal with them. If you don't deal with them, how can you expect to get the business?

Very often, avoiding the prospect's concerns is what leaves the sales professional without a transaction, scratching his head and wondering what went wrong. This is very often when the salesman says to himself (or to others) things like, "We had such good rapport. I don't know why he didn't go with us," or, "The woman agreed with everything I had to say, and she felt we were offering a great package. It's beyond me why we didn't get the business."

As a rule, if a prospect agrees with everything you say and doesn't dispute or challenge anything, that right there is a red flag!

TAKE INTO ACCOUNT THE *"HUMAN ELEMENT:"* KNOW AND RESPECT YOUR TENDENCIES

"Know Thyself"
—TEMPLE OF APOLLO AT DELPHI

I am a big proponent of the philosophy *"play to your strengths."* Spend less time trying to fix what you're bad at and more time honing what you're already talented at. If you haven't already accepted this particular fact about life, let me remind you and make it absolutely clear: *You are not going to be great at everything!*

Even if you are an extremely multifaceted individual with many diverse talents and a true sense of the Renaissance, you will not be great at *everything*. Please just be open to that. Da Vinci was perhaps the most diversely talented individual known to mankind, but even he wasn't great at everything.

Even if, hypothetically, you were the anomaly in the entire human race and possessed the potential to be great at every single thing you took on, would you really want to concern yourself with all of it? Would you even have time for it? Or would you be better served by focusing on one thing, or just a small collection of specific skills, that you could truly excel at and that were clearly most important to you?

Observe the patterns that—over time—point to what you are good at and what you enjoy, and then play to that. For example, I have come to accept that while I genuinely consider myself to be one of the more gifted sales professionals you are ever going to come across, I am not particularly good at handling administrative details. As a matter of fact, I am a downright poor administrator.

So, do you think I spend the majority of my time working on my skills as an administrator, so I can improve this area that is a weakness of mine and catch up? Absolutely not! I delegate and hand-off those responsibilities to people who are far better at it than I, and who are getting paid for it.

Next, you are about to read something that is counter to what you have probably heard a lot of the "gurus" say in the past, but it is a clear example of taking the human element into account. *Allow time for procrastination!* Yes, you read that correctly. I didn't say you have to eliminate procrastination or that you cannot be successful if there are times when you procrastinate.

Sometimes procrastination will demand its space—for whatever reason. Personally, I know that sometimes I am simply not ready to get crackin' or ready to step into the zone until I've had time to acclimatize to my environment, warm up or get organized. If I forced myself to do the intended work when I'm in the space I've just described, a part of me would say, *"Forget this!* I'm out of here. I don't need this*,"* or something to that effect. Let's just say that *"forget"* might not be the "F" word I would actually use.

For example, before I sat down to write this chapter, which involves thinking creatively and being able to lay down my ideas in a way that is concise and flows smoothly for the reader, I did a lot of walking. I was out and about in New York City in the middle of June, and there was a major parade going on today. By the time I got to the library where I am writing this, I was hot and sweaty. I had been fighting crowds of people simply to be able to walk and was feeling a bit low on energy. Perhaps you've been there yourself.

If I had just sat down to write, without any acclimation time, do you think I would have been at my best? I can already tell you I would not have been. So what did I do? I got a cup of iced tea, I freshened up, I sent out a few overdue emails, I gave the air conditioning some time to cool me down, and I reviewed a couple of newsletters I had written recently. That whole process took around twenty to twenty-five minutes. When I finally began writing, I was in the zone and ready to rock!

Instead of attempting to completely eliminate procrastination in your life, focus on spending *less* time procrastinating. For example, I personally find it difficult to get work done when my workspace is in disarray and I'm not organized. Call it a pet peeve, a compulsion, or whatever you'd like.

So if I sit down to work and things are not together, I will organize what needs to be organized so *I can be productive and have everything I need.* But I also won't allow it to turn into a complete cleaning expedition of my entire office or think that I need everything to be spotless or in place before moving forward.

That is the difference between spending five to ten minutes procrastinating versus thirty minutes or more. Big difference!

And this brings me to another important point. Focus on making your procrastination **"productive procrastination."** No, this is not an oxymoron.

For example, if you sit down to do some work and you realize—for whatever reason—you're just not ready to get crackin' yet, instead of picking up the phone to call a friend or going on YouTube to check out a music video, why not spend some time cleaning up your desktop or one of your email boxes? Why not check out a training video or listen to an audio program that is relevant to your business? Why not organize your workspace or prepare an outline for the next day?

Are they still forms of procrastination? Yes. But at least they are putting you in a mode to be more effective and more productive, and they are things you would have needed to do at some point anyway.

In addition, when you are focused on a particular project or outcome, allow *time* for the human element. Is it possible that, at some point, you will need a break? Is it possible that, at some point—even for a little while—you may get distracted or overwhelmed by something? Is it possible something or someone may get you pissed off or disappointed, and you will need some time to clear your head?

If you have answered *"no"* to all of those questions, then there is a good chance you are not human. In the world of time management, we call this creating *"buffer time."* Whatever you want to call it, I encourage you to make this practice a consistent part of your repertoire.

Work your tail off, stay committed and do whatever it takes to create the results you so badly desire, but in the process understand that you are human, and it will serve you well to treat yourself accordingly. Even Pete Rose took the occasional day off.

REVIEW:

- The mastermind principle, first coined by Napoleon Hill in the 1930s, is defined as, "Coordination of knowledge and effort, in a spirit of harmony between two or more people, for the attainment of a definite purpose."
- A part of surrounding yourself with people who are truly committed to your growth and who want to see you succeed is first distancing yourself from people who, despite what they might say outwardly, do *not* want to see you succeed.
- The people who would hold you back are very often planted within your own "camp" or inner circle of friends and family.
- Be willing to answer a question with a question.
- Keep your mind centered.
- Have fun with your mistakes.
- Go to the seminars.
- Always look for what's beyond the words.
- Establishing credibility is crucial.
- Create urgency.
- Be willing to hear your prospect's honest opinion.
- Take into account the "human element"–know and respect your tendencies.

10

THE FORTUNE IS IN THE FOLLOW THROUGH

YOU MUST STAY THE COURSE

At the end of the day, that is what truly matters.

Everything I am sharing with you in this book is only as useful and relevant as the degree to which you take it and *use* it!

This is not extremely complicated, but it is absolutely vital. The real question here is, how are you going to take what I have covered and put it into practice out there in the real world? That is what separates the people who really step up and excel from those who simply stagnate or tread water.

It amazes me how many people will buy a book of this kind—actually spend the money to order it—and then never even read it. A smaller percentage will take the time to read it, but then never do anything with the tools they've learned. An even smaller percentage will take the time to read it, do the exercises and play full out, but after all that many still won't actually take the skills and approaches I am sharing here and put them into practice. They let it drop!

Have you ever fallen prey to patterns of behavior like that yourself in the past? At one time or another, we *all* have.

So, what is it going to take to follow through? Well, in my experience, when looking to figure out the best approach in any area, it is wise to first understand what *not* to do or what does not work. That can save you a lot of time and frustration. So let's first take a look at what *not to do*—what to avoid.

In general, the **five most common mistakes** people make that keep them from moving forward or accomplishing their intended outcomes in *anything* are:

1. Not being clear on their **outcome.** Most people don't really know what they want. They have a general idea, but they're not really clear.
2. Not being clear on a **strategy.** They just wing it and shoot from the hip— hoping that what they are doing will work or be effective.
3. They don't take **sufficient action.** If they do have a strategy, they don't actually execute it and put it into effect.
4. They don't pay attention to what is **working** and **what is not**— often repeating mistakes or flawed strategies.
5. **They don't get help** from outside sources—ego; the *"I can do it all on my own"* syndrome.

Does any of this strike a chord?

Let's take a look at these five factors and how they relate to you. It is my hope and wish that you embrace how this relates to your life and the results that you create. This is truly where the rubber meets the road.

NOT BEING CLEAR ON YOUR OUTCOME

Let me put it this way: if you're not clear, you need to get clear! And I don't mean just a general idea. To go back to the travel analogy, imagine if I set out to meet a family member who lived in Florida and I wasn't clear on what city? That would be a rather interesting trip. But I could tell others exactly where I'm headed. I could say, "Hey, I'm going to Florida!"

I'm not saying that your vision of what you want to create for yourself should not or cannot change along the way. Of course it can, and often that will be what makes the journey exciting—rediscovering and reinventing yourself as you go. But when beginning the journey, at least be clear on your original destination so you have a definite direction to move in.

In some of my consulting programs, I conduct a very powerful and comprehensive workshop on goal setting, which not only gets you crystal clear on exactly what you want to accomplish over the next twelve months of your life along with a game plan and strategy, but which also helps you identify and literally break through what has been holding you back up to that point.

This frees up participants to move beyond those barriers and take massive action to accomplish the things they want most. The main reason I conduct that program is because I believe it is an absolutely critical step in the process of creating success in any endeavor—whether it's one project in particular or your life as a whole.

Not being crystal clear on your outcome and what could possibly stand in your way is **huge!**

NOT BEING CLEAR ON YOUR STRATEGY

"Do you know what they call someone who is really excited with no skill? They call that person dangerous."
–Tony Robbins

Make sure you have a game plan, or a strategy in place. The key here is to not worry about whether or not it's *perfect*. Don't get caught up in the *"paralysis of analysis."* As referenced above, you can always enhance and improve your plan as you move along the path. But you must put *something* in place.

When I consider how many times I've changed the structure of my company's business model since its original inception, it makes me want to laugh out loud. And thank God I did. If I had not, I would be operating from an outdated, ineffective model and leaving tremendous amounts of money and contributions on the table.

If, as you read this book, you are engaged in a major project or working towards a particular outcome, and you do not have a clear-cut strategy or game plan, you might want to put this book down right now and create one. I'm not joking. A few minutes of effective planning can save you days, weeks or even years of time, energy and frustration. Don't let the fact that you might already be in action around something prevent you from taking a step back and charting a better course.

If you're not sure how to do that or if you want to make sure you do a good job of it (notice I didn't say "perfect"), there are plenty of people out there who can assist you in that. These days, there are plenty of strategic consultants, executive coaches, career counselors, workshops, seminars and more to assist you in doing exactly that (including my company). You simply need to reach out and get the help.

Regarding the idea of getting help... more on that in a bit.

The next ingredient is the glue that connects any idea, any concept I will ever share with you:

IT'S SIMPLE: YOU MUST TAKE *SUFFICIENT* ACTION!

I almost feel foolish writing this down because it is so blatantly obvious.

But the bottom line is that it must be emphasized! Taking action is a classic example of something that makes so much sense and seems so simple, yet so many people struggle with actually executing on it effectively. Now in the heading above, notice I didn't just say that you must take action—I said you must take *sufficient* action. There is a big difference.

There have been many examples of people throughout history who have taken action and yet never succeeded! They never achieved the goals, outcomes and dreams they laid out for themselves. They never seemed to quite finish the story.

That is because simply taking action is one thing, but taking consistent, effective and sufficient action to make your vision a reality is a completely different animal. This means executing your plan even when you don't feel like it; moving ahead and honoring your word to yourself, even when the outcome seems in doubt; going above and beyond to do whatever it takes—regardless of what that may bring up for you.

When talking about taking sufficient action to achieve an intended outcome, there is a distinction you must consider that is absolutely critical, because very often this will single-handedly determine whether or not you follow through to completion like a true samurai and come home with the victory. It is this: you must come from a place that your intended goal or outcome is an absolute *must*, versus simply a *should*. In other words: "I *must* do this; I *have* to find a way to get this done. This must happen! I will do *whatever it takes* to make this a reality!" as opposed to "I *should* make that call, I *should* go to the gym, I *should* follow up..." etc.

When you hear someone say "I should make that call," or "I should follow through..." how powerful—how clear—does that sound? Does that sound like true commitment? *Not even for a moment!* Remember this expression: "When you *should* too much, you *should* all over yourself."

Now, why is it not just helpful but *critical* that you come from a place of *must* versus *should*?

In my experience, with close to twenty years of studying and analyzing human behavior, as well as teaching and coaching people from many different walks of life on how to perform at their best and truly take life for everything that it is worth, I have identified one central, unifying reason for this: very simply put, like it or not, *setbacks and adversities are going to occur along the way to any major goal.* No matter how well you prepare, no matter how many things you do right, no matter how hard you work, no matter how smart you think you are, at some point events beyond your control are going to get in the way and you are going to hit a wall. You're going to be knocked on your ass—and your conviction is going to be tested.

I have yet to hear of one single long-term success story where that has not had happened at least once, if not many times. And it is in those key, critical moments of setback and frustration that a goal or commitment considered a *should*—something you're just interested in—is simply not going to be enough. **It needs to be a *must*, or you will fold!**

PAYING ATTENTION TO WHAT IS WORKING, AND WHAT IS NOT

Assuming you possess the conviction and drive I have referred to above, and assuming you are coming from a place of *"must,"* I am here to tell you that unfortunately (or fortunately) that is not enough. It is critical, but it is not the entire package. To be an individual who follows through consistently and effectively, you need more.

You need to be **flexible.** *Flexibility.* You need to pay close attention to what's working and what isn't and adjust your strategy accordingly. At times, this requires a willingness to roll with the punches and let go of pre-existing agendas or attachments when it seems that fate has a plan all its own. You hang in and you *adjust* your approach.

When considering this, I always like to reference the metaphor of the oak tree and a blade of grass. This one's been around for a while, and with good reason. I have yet to hear a better example of the sheer power of flexibility.

Compare a full-grown oak tree to a mere blade of grass. Which one looks stronger and more powerful? Clearly, it's the mighty oak. It is exponentially larger, thicker and harder, and it towers over all the blades of grass that surround it. Yes?

Yet when confronted with a violent storm that unleashes powerful winds and turbulence for hours at a time, which of the two is more likely to withstand the pressure and remain standing? It's simple, the blade of grass. Why? Because the blade of grass is **flexible.**

It naturally bends and sways from side to side in obedience to the wind. The oak, on the other hand, is too hard and rigid to be flexible. As a result, even with all of its power and strength, the oak runs a much larger risk of being knocked down or uprooted. And very often this is exactly what happens.

Be like a blade of grass.

This topic of taking sufficient action and staying the course, observing what works and what doesn't, being flexible and unflappable, inevitably brings me to the attribute of **emotional resiliency.** I'd like to bring your attention to what I consider to be the *single most devastating blow* that can be delivered to anyone's self-confidence and personal momentum—one of the biggest barriers to anyone's progress. That is not a claim I make lightly. So please pay extra careful attention to this. It is:

When you let *yourself* down. When you don't show up for yourself.

Just take that in for a moment.

You see, when things outside of your control occur, that's one thing. You can stamp your feet, get indignant, rebel and talk about everything that's unfair and what you're going to do about it. But when you let yourself down, it's a completely different experience.

Who *ultimately* is responsible for your circumstances and where you end up in life?

You are!

What I'm referring to here is when you let yourself down by committing to yourself—upon everything you're worth, upon everything that's holy to you, upon *who you are*—to take certain actions and follow through, and then you *don't!*

These are the times you need to walk your talk, when so much is relying on this that you *have* to follow through, and yet you *do not.* For example, being late for key meetings, oversleeping, not getting into the office or class when you said you would, not preparing in advance the way you know you should have, snapping at others who are only trying to help you, or maybe just not doing the work, period.

This is a great opportunity to be brutally honest with yourself and confront both the reality and the responsibility of this aspect of life, and everything you make it mean. Consider for a moment how different it is when you have no one else to blame but *yourself*—when you are the sole culprit and perpetrator of the mess you are in or the evils you are suffering; or when, had you treated someone *else* the way you just treated *yourself*, that person would be justified in ending the friendship or never really trusting you again.

This applies as much to the world of sales as it does anything else in life. I have found that in any selling situation, there is what happened, and then there is your *interpretation* of what happened. And these can be two completely different experiences.

I can tell you that personally, in the past when I first began in sales, if I gave a presentation that didn't get the result or was presented with objections that I did not successfully handle, getting rejected or not getting the order wasn't the only thing that would upset me. Obviously, I wanted to get the order or create the relationship, but what really bothered me was when I immediately focused on what I did wrong, what I *should* have done better, or what mistakes I made that cost me the sale. I would think that if I had just done a few things a bit differently or had been just a bit more on the ball, it would have been in the bag. That's what would drive me *crazy*!

Learning from one's mistakes and identifying how you can be better next time is one thing. Dwelling on what went wrong and indulging in all of the negativity and self-judgment that goes along with that is something entirely different.

Early in my career I experienced patterns of self-sabotage—of *"snatching defeat out of the jaws of victory,"* as they say. That is an enlightening and truly humbling experience to go through. I've been through those experiences more times than I care to confess. And I'll be the first to admit, there have been mistakes I've had to repeat once, twice, or more, before I finally got it and learned my lesson.

But here's the thing:

It's in that exact moment of personal let down—of self doubt and silent desperation—when you think, *"Man, it can't get any worse than this,"* or *"How could I have screwed that up so badly? I have no one else to blame but myself,"* that you must dig even deeper and be willing do three simple things. This three-step process I would like to share with you, which has gotten me through some of the greatest personal let downs of my life, can be used to move beyond any adversity—external or self-inflicted. So please sit up straight and open your eyes a bit wider as you read this. You must:

1. **ENDURE**
2. **FORGIVE**
3. **GET BACK ON TRACK**

ENDURANCE

"Weeping may endureth for a night. But joy cometh in the morning."
—PSALMS 30

The power of endurance is magical. Sometimes you endure simply for the sake of enduring—because it beats the alternative. You do *whatever it takes* to hang on and hang in.

The most profound teachings I have ever read on the topic of endurance were written by my friend and mentor Chin Ning Chu, in her book *Thick Face, Black Heart.* Instead of attempting to interpret it or give it my own spin, I'd like to share a few quotes from the chapter entitled "The Magical Power of Endurance"

> *"What makes a great one great? It is not that he possesses the image of the knight in shining armor like St. George slaying the dragon. Such an image has been held dear by the executives who are climbing the corporate ladders. What makes one truly great is knowing how to suffer the insufferable and how to endure the unendurable.*
> *Everyone knows how to thrive in the good times. It is the trying times that separate the one who has substance from the one who merely possesses the image. Through trials and tribulations, one endures by enduring. Thus, the human spirit triumphs over itself."*

And:

> *"Without the strength to endure the crisis, we will not see the opportunity within. It is within the process of endurance that opportunity reveals itself. Opportunity always exists within a*

crisis situation, but when we lose heart in a devastating crisis, we are blinded by our own emotion. When we can calmly endure the unendurable, the opportunity for a better alternative surfaces and reveals itself."

Are you getting this?

"...the human spirit triumphs over itself." I love it!

Simply put, like it or not, you are going to be tested. In a big way! Whether it comes from external unexpected thunderbolts or through your own imperfections, for whatever reason, that seems to be the way of things.

How will you handle it when that test comes? How can you realistically expect to attain victory if you do not possess the ability to endure the *"unendurable?"*

"Among one's affairs there should not be more than two or three matters of what one could call great concern. If these are deliberated upon during ordinary times, they can be understood. Thinking about things previously and then handling them lightly when the time comes is what this is all about. To face an event and solve it lightly is difficult if you are not resolved beforehand, and there will always be uncertainty in hitting your mark."

HAGAKURE, *THE BOOK OF THE SAMURAI*

FORGIVENESS

"If we were to cast aside every man who had made a mistake once, useful (people) could probably not come by. A (person) who makes a mistake once will be considerably more prudent and useful because of his repentance."

HAGAKURE, *THE BOOK OF THE SAMURAI*

Forgiveness, of yourself and others. If you want to talk about a cleansing, purifying, and empowering emotion that is spoken about in virtually every religion on the face of the planet, it is forgiveness.

It's in that moment of self-judgment, humiliation and fear—perhaps fear of the future, fear that you won't have what it takes, fear that you're not good enough, fear that you'll screw up again, or many other possible strains of fear when you are confronted with the reality of all your imperfections, every bad decision you have ever made, every display of insanity you have ever shown yourself—that *you must find the willingness within yourself to forgive yourself.*

I want to remind you of something. And you might want to put down the book and contemplate this next statement for a few moments:

It's okay! You are doing the best you can. It's not always easy, and you have a lot to be proud of.

I encourage you to repeat that statement to yourself in the first person a few times. Have you ever found that it is much easier to forgive other people than it is to forgive yourself? Are you open from this moment forward, perhaps for the rest of your life, to giving yourself the same kind of access and entitlement to the amazing emotion of forgiveness as you would to someone else?

There is something else to remember regarding your willingness to forgive. When you hold onto resentment, anger, guilt or whatever emotions may accompany a lack of forgiveness—whether towards yourself or others—it can be very unhealthy. It can affect you mentally, emotionally and even *physically.* Think about how powerful that is.

I feel the following three paragraphs, written by Eckhart Tolle in his book *The Power of Now* express this experience as well as anything I have ever read. He refers to the field of negative energy that fills your body and infiltrates your health as "the pain body." I encourage you to read every word below as if it's gold:

"In a fully functional organism, an emotion has a very short life span. It is like a momentary ripple or wave on the surface of your being. When you are not in your body, however, an emotion can survive inside you for days or weeks, or

join with other emotions of a similar frequency that have merged and become the pain body, a parasite that can live inside you for years, feed on your energy, lead to physical illness, and make your life miserable.

So place your attention on feeling the emotion, and check whether your mind is holding on to a grievance pattern such as blame, self-pity or resentment that is feeding the emotion. If that is the case, it means you haven't forgiven.

Non-forgiveness is often toward another person or yourself, but it may just as well be toward any situation or condition—past, present or future—that your mind refuses to accept... Forgiveness is to relinquish your grievance and so to let go of grief. It happens naturally once you realize that your grievance serves no purpose except to strengthen a false sense of self. Forgiveness is to offer no resistance to life—to allow life to live through you. The alternatives are pain and suffering, a greatly restricted flow of life energy, and in many cases physical disease."

You endure, you forgive, you wipe the slate clean and you start anew.

Then ... you **get back on track!**

GETTING BACK ON TRACK

"No matter what it is, there is nothing that cannot be done. If one manifests the determination, he can move heaven and earth as he pleases."

HAGAKURE, *THE BOOK OF THE SAMURAI*

Simply put, you get back up and you make that next phone call, you shake that next hand, you set that next appointment, you give that next presentation, you ask for that next listing, your write that next policy, you create that next proposal, you continue to put yourself out there and *ask* for what you *know* is right and for what you know will help other people! And lo and behold, by doing this eventually you actually generate some results and you *get back on track.*

With those results, you generate some *momentum.* And with that momentum, you take even more *action.* And with that action, you generate more *results* and more momentum, and take more action—and the cycle continues until you have created an *upward spiral* in your life! And this continues: successes begin to stack upon one another, victory after victory after victory, until you get to a place where you have completely elevated the quality of your life!

You have created a new self-concept where you are operating at a level that, at one point, you only dreamt of. At one point, it was merely an idea, a vague notion in your mind—and now you are living it as a reality!

I'm talking about where the greatest dreams you once had become a mere shadow of the life you are actually living. Those moments where you wake up and say, "Man, there *must* be a God or *something* out there, because my life feels just too good for this to be of my own doing!"

I'm here to remind you that it's possible and it happens every day. *Every day!* Make no mistake. It happened in my life. It's happened in the lives of so many more people than you realize. I know so many vice presidents and company owners, top producers, managing directors, presidents, CEOs, cutting-edge entrepreneurs—people who have come from much more challenging circumstances in the past (much of which was self-inflicted) to be where they are today. **You *endure*, you *forgive* and you *get back on track*.** And that right there, my friend, has been the genesis of some of the greatest success stories throughout history.

THE STORY OF BRUCE

I'd like to share a true story that I feel clearly illustrates this process. It's the story of a gentleman who for now, we'll just call Bruce.

I like Bruce right out of the gates, because like myself, Bruce is a Brooklyn boy. But he's a local boy who did well. He got himself into Harvard Business School. No small feat. Now in case you don't already know, anyone who graduates with an MBA from Harvard has pretty much written themselves a golden ticket for the rest of their professional lives. It doesn't mean that everything is handed to you on a silver platter. But let's just say it creates some pretty amazing opportunities and opens doors that very few people are ever able to walk through. And he was there, at the pinnacle, if you will.

But then something very unique and strange happened to Bruce. He developed a severe mental block where he had trouble reading, writing and focusing. He simply was unable to concentrate. Now, a regular university is difficult enough to get a degree at. Can you imagine how competitive, how much pressure there must be for students in Harvard Business School? And all of the ego and jostling that goes along with that?

In the midst of that, he couldn't function like his normal self. He tried and tried, but he was blocked. So at a certain point, when he realized it wasn't working, the unthinkable happened. He dropped out of Harvard Business School. So close to the prize, and he had to drop out!

For many people, that would have been game over, at least professionally. To be at such a high level and then to fall off? And he did hit a "bottom" for a while, if you'd like to call it that. He lived as kind of a professional nomad.

He worked as a piano man like Billy Joel, playing at bars for tips. He tried doing some writing. He even drove a taxi in New York City. You know, one of the yellow cabs. Formerly at Harvard Business School, then driving a cab. Talk about going from one to the other extreme. I guess you could say professionally he was lost.

But here's what's interesting: he endured, he picked himself up and he got back on track. He got into trading stocks and it turned out that he had a penchant for it. He was a natural and a genius in that area. He could see patterns and market trends that others could not.

So he delved into it, and he continued to thrive and created an investment fund. He did so well at it, that he began to attract the attention of high net worth investors and institutions. And he continued on and started to raise some big-time assets.

He eventually got to a point where his hedge fund was managing over $14 billion dollars! Yes, that's billion with a B. I wonder how many former cab drivers have managed 14 billion dollar hedge funds.

Finally in March of 2014, he sold his fund for 4.8 billion dollars. Which essentially became his personal net worth.

The gentleman I'm talking about is named Bruce Kovner and the fund he created is called Caxton Associates. He's obviously on the Forbes 400 list of wealthiest individuals. New York Magazine once called him the most powerful New Yorker that you've never heard of. In 2013 he gave a gift to the Julliard School in New York for $60 million. Thanks Bruce!

He endured, he forgave himself or whatever he had to do, and he got back on track.

When you think about what Mr. Kovner endured to create the level of success that he has, do you think perhaps that you can come in to the office a bit earlier, work a bit harder, beat on your craft, master your skills? Do you think you can attack sales resistance and hearing the word "no" with a passion? Can you do whatever it takes to master your sales game and become a true "Samurai of Sales?"

CONCLUSION

If I had to choose between possessing raw talent and having the ability to be unrelenting in my follow through, I would opt for the latter any day of the week. It is like the water on the rock. With consistent application over extended periods of time, eventually the laws of nature must adhere to your persistence. It truly is not a sprint; it is a marathon. Stay the course, be true to your convictions, and above all else **follow through and make it stick!**

REVIEW:

- Anything you learn in this book is only as useful and relevant as the degree to which you take it and use it.
- When attempting a task, the five most common mistakes people make that keep them from moving forward or accomplishing their intended outcomes are:
  1. Not being clear on their outcome
  2. Not being clear on their strategy
  3. Not taking sufficient action
  4. Not paying attention to what is working and what is not
  5. Not getting help when they need it

- Very often the setbacks you impose upon yourself can be the most debilitating of all.
- The three key steps in moving past any adversity, external or self-inflicted are:
  1. You Endure
  2. You Forgive
  3. You Get Back On Track
- Very often, you endure simply to endure. Because not enduring would be even worse.
- As a rule over the long term, persistence and following through will win out over simply having talent any day of the week.

FINAL THOUGHTS

Human life is truly a short affair. It is better to live doing the things that you like. It is foolish to live within this dream of a world seeing unpleasantness and doing only things that you do not like.
HAGAKURE, *THE BOOK OF THE SAMURAI*

As you can tell by my writing style throughout this entire book, I like to get to the point quickly and speak to what I believe is most important. I will make no exception in my final thoughts.

What I truly want you to understand on a deep gut level is that *it is a true gift and privilege to be in professional sales.* You have the opportunity to create so much for yourself in terms of income, a sense of pride, satisfaction, and contribution to others. You also have the opportunity to live a unique and interesting life in which there are always new people to meet, new experiences to have, new lessons to learn and new challenges to overcome.

Perhaps no occupation epitomizes this truth more clearly than that of being in professional sales. For the record, *I love sales!* I love doing it, thinking about it, being a member of this proud community and all the benefits it has to offer. I tell you from experience—I urge you; I plead with you—that whatever you have to do, whatever you must be willing to take on or sacrifice, do whatever it takes to become a **sales samurai – a true master.** *The rewards are inexplicable!*

I think the best way to express my thoughts on this topic is to share with you a newsletter I sent to my database years ago after getting inspired early on a Saturday morning. I believe this describes rather clearly how I feel about the privilege of being an entrepreneur and anyone who has made the commitment to read this book in its entirety—and why it truly is worth it to do whatever it takes to attain sales mastery. Enjoy.

MITCH HARRIS NEWSLETTER, DECEMBER 2007

Recently I woke up early on a Saturday morning before sunrise. Perhaps you know that feeling of being up early on a weekend morning—serene and peaceful, in a way it never is during the week. I decided to go for a brief walk in my midtown Manhattan neighborhood before getting onto my computer for the day.

After looking east and staring at the United Nations for a few minutes, thinking about everything that building symbolizes and the significance of what occurs only two blocks from my home, I looked across the East River beyond the U.N. and noticed the morning sun that was about to break through a scattering of clouds above the Citibank building in Queens.

I then turned west in the opposite direction and could see straight down 42nd Street, all the way to Times Square. The lights of Madame Tussauds wax museum and several other stores were still blinking brightly, even at this hour. I looked to my right and saw the world famous Chrysler building standing proudly as well—fully lit.

As I pondered how incredible a city Manhattan is and how truly amazing this life we're given can be, I began thinking about several articles I had recently read in a business magazine. They told stories of various entrepreneurs who had created immense fortunes and had come up with inventions and technological innovations that were impacting the way people lived and the business world in general. And I began to think about how much incredible opportunity and potential is orbiting all around us at any given moment. There is so much here for us to take!

If you are an entrepreneur or sales professional of any kind, you have created a tremendous opportunity for yourself. You have put yourself onto a platform that has the ability to catapult you to incredible heights of accomplishment and fulfillment.

So just a reminder to those of you who may be in the throes of your business right now: when you feel that tinge of doubt or fear that inevitably comes along with the unpredictable nature of being an entrepreneur, remember, this is absolutely the game you want to be playing! You are here to do big things, live a life of significance and create incredible wealth and fulfillment for yourself and the people you care about.

I applaud you for your courage and ambition and I am proud to have you as a fellow member of my community: the community of entrepreneurs, people who are willing to take risks and make things happen—people who have the courage to let their results and personal performance dictate their rewards.

When you think about it, would you really want to be living any other way?

Once again, I thank you for the time and the trust you have put into reading this book. I hope we have the opportunity to meet in person at one of my live events, or that you can join me on a webinar sometime soon. I also encourage you to get onto my mailing list if you have not already so we can stay in touch. God Bless, best of luck and go close some business!

Yours in living a fulfilled life,

Mitch Harris

"The Samurai of Sales"

ABOUT THE AUTHOR:
MITCH HARRIS

Mitch Harris, aka "The Samurai of Sales," has been helping companies to increase their production and achieve greater profitability for over fifteen years. He has traveled all over the United States and as far as Hong Kong to do this work and has worked with some of the largest corporations on the planet.

But Mitch also thrives on helping small- to mid-sized companies step up and get to that ever-so-crucial next level. He has been a guest and keynote speaker for a very diverse group of organizations and is passionate about being of service and helping others.

Mitch lives in New York City, but travels often—both for business and leisure. He is also an avid swimmer, practitioner of Vipassana meditation and a weekend musician.

If you would like to explore bringing Mitch in to help your company increase sales and get to the next level, or you have an interest in bringing in Mitch to speak as a guest or keynote speaker, please feel free to contact us at:

mitch@samuraiofsales.com
www.samuraiofsales.com
212-682-4754

Feel free to contact us as well if you'd like to explore the application process for becoming a member of the **"Your Sales Breakthrough!"** coaching and mastermind program, or working with a personal business coach.

If you would like to purchase additional copies of the *Samurai Of Sales* print book or audio program, please fill out the order form behind this page and send in to us, or visit our website.

For large bulk or corporate product orders, feel free to contact us directly.

Bulk savings packages are available.

Register for our free newsletter at: www.samuraiofsales.com

QUICK ORDER FORM

Fax Orders: 917-338-2548. Send this form.

Telephone Orders: Call 212-682-4754. Have your credit card ready.

Email Orders: mitch@samuraiofsales.com

Postal Orders: Communication Mastery, Inc. 320 East 42nd Street, Suite 215, New York, NY 10017

Please send the following products. I have specified quantities and current market prices. I understand that I may return any of them for a full refund within 30 days, for any reason:

_____

_____

_____

_____

_____

_____

Please send more FREE information on:

- Other Books
- Speaking/Seminars
- Mailing Lists
- Consulting
- Video Training
- Networking

Name:_____

Address: _____

City:_____State:____Zip:_____Telephone:_____

Email Address:_____

Credit Card: VISA, M/C, AMEX, DISC

Card #:_____Exp:_____Sec:_____

Signature:_____

Checks made payable to: Communication Mastery, Inc.

Shipping by air

U.S.: $3.95 for first book and $2.00 for each additional book. $5.95 for each audio book and $4.00 for each additional. Bulk rates are available

International: $13.00 for first book or disc; $9.00 for each additional product (estimate). Bulk rates are available.

Morgan James
Speakers Group

We connect Morgan James published
authors with live and online events
and audiences who will benefit
from their expertise.